The
WORD of GOD
and the
MIND of MAN

The
WORD of GOD
and the
MIND of MAN

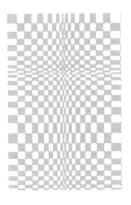

Ronald H. Nash
Western Kentucky University

ZONDERVAN
PUBLISHING HOUSE
OF THE ZONDERVAN CORPORATION
GRAND RAPIDS, MICHIGAN 49506

THE WORD OF GOD AND THE MIND OF MAN
Copyright © 1982 by The Zondervan Corporation
Grand Rapids, Michigan

Library of Congress Cataloging in Publication Data

Nash, Ronald H.
  The word of God and the mind of man.

  Includes bibliographical references and indexes.
    1. Knowledge, Theory of (Religion)—Addresses, essays, lectures. 2. Revelation—
Addresses, essays, lectures. I. Title.
BT50.N37 1982   231'.042   82-13495
ISBN 0-310-45131-0

Edited by Jack Stewart and Ben Chapman
Designed by Louise Bauer

Printed in the United States of America

82 83 84 85 86 87 88 — 10 9 8 7 6 5 4 3 2 1

To
four who helped along the way

John L. Benson
Terrelle Crum
James Godley, Sr.
Carlton Gregory

Contents

◆

Preface

◆

The title of this book can be understood in at least two ways. First of all, *The Word of God and the Mind of Man* is an exploration of the extent to which the human mind can receive and understand divine revelation, insofar as this revelation is understood to include the communication of truth. On a second and more fundamental level, the phrase *the word of God* recalls its classical context—the prologue to John's gospel and the classical Logos doctrine of the early church fathers: all human knowledge is possible because of the unique human participation in the eternal Logos of God, Jesus Christ.

Some readers may also wonder if the affinity of the title to one of Karl Barth's early books, *The Word of God and the Word of Man*, is intentional. It is, in the sense that the positions advocated in this book are offered in conscious opposition to those contemporary theologians who maintain that human words are incapable of carrying a cognitive word of God.

The views I explain and defend in this book are an important foundation of what has been the mainstream of evangelical thinking about divine revelation and religious epistemology since the end of World War II. It is the first book that attempts to trace this position back to its roots; a systematic examination of the theoretical foundations and historical development of this position is not available elsewhere. Since many Evangelicals are beginning to drift from the former consensus about the indispensability and legitimacy of a belief in cognitive or propositional revelation, a fresh examination of this view and its major competition can be helpful at this particular time in the history of the church.

A number of people read all or parts of the manuscript and offered helpful suggestions and criticisms. They include Robert Johnston, Arvin Vos, William Lane, Julius Scott, Gordon Clark, Larry Mayhew, Robert Roberts, James Spiceland, and Edward Schoen. Stan Gundry of Zondervan and his editorial staff suggested several changes that improved the original manuscript.

Chapter 6 was originally presented as a lecture to a meeting of the Biblical Theology Society at Tyndale House, Cambridge, England. It was subsequently published (in somewhat different and extended form than it appears here) in *The Westminster Theological Journal* (1977). Other sections of the book have appeared in articles published in *Christianity Today*, *The New Scholasticism*, and *Augustinian Studies*. Several paragraphs also appeared previously in my essay, "Gordon Clark's Theory of Knowledge," which appeared in *The Philosophy of Gordon H. Clark* (Philadelphia: Presbyterian and Reformed, 1968). In each case, the permission to reprint is acknowledged with appreciation.

Introduction: The Unknown God

The last two centuries of Christian theology are the record of an evolving attack on the role of knowledge in the Christian faith. Following the lead of the eighteenth-century philosophers David Hume and Immanuel Kant, many modern theologians have questioned God's ability to communicate truth to man and undermined man's ability to attain knowledge about God.

Gordon Kaufman typifies this agnostic attitude toward God:

> The real reference for "God" is never accessible to us or in any way open to our observation or experience. It must remain always an unknown X, a mere limiting idea with no content. It stands for the fact that God transcends our knowledge in modes and ways of which we can never be aware and of which we have no inkling.[1]

Kaufman does not stop with the suggestion that the being referred to by the word *God* is an unknown X. He adds: "God is ultimately profound Mystery and utterly escapes our every effort to grasp or comprehend him. Our concepts are at best metaphors and symbols of his being, not literally applicable."[2]

Modern scepticism about the possibility of attaining knowledge about God is illustrated in the writings of philosopher W. T. Stace who maintained that "God is utterly and forever beyond the reach of the logical intellect or of any intellectual comprehension, and that in consequence when we try to comprehend his nature intellectually, con-

---

[1]Gordon D. Kaufman, *God the Problem* (Cambridge: Harvard University Press, 1972), p. 95.
[2]Ibid., p. 95.

tradictions appear in our thinking."[3] While Stace regarded himself as neither a theologian nor a Christian in the traditional sense, comments similar to his appear in the writings of many modern theologians. According to Stace, while God cannot be known by the human intellect,

> he can be known in direct religious or mystical experience. Perhaps this is much the same as saying that he can be known by "faith" but not by "reason." Any attempt to reach God through logic, through the conceptual, logical intellect, is doomed, comes up against an absolute barrier; but this does not mean the death of religion—it does not mean that there is no possibility of that knowledge and communion with God which religion requires. It means that the knowledge of God which is the essence of religion is not of an intellectual kind. It is rather the direct experience of the mystic himself. Or if we are not mystics, then it is whatever it is that you would call religious experience. And this experience of God-in-the-heart, shall we say, is not an intellectual understanding or explanation—this experience of God is the essence of religion.[4]

What Kaufman, the Christian theologian, and Stace, the non-Christian mystic, and thousands of theologians, seminary professors, and pastors share in common is the trivialization or repudiation of the traditional role that *truth* has played in the Christian religion. Cognitive knowledge about God is simply declared impossible and replaced by personal encounter, religious feeling, trust, or obedience. In the words of John Baillie, "God does not give us information by communication. He gives us Himself in communion. It is not information about God that is revealed but . . . God Himself."[5] Or as William Temple once put it: "There is no such thing as revealed truth. . . . What is offered to man's apprehension in any specific revelation is not truth concerning God but the living God Himself."[6]

The theological agnosticism represented by Kaufman, Baillie, and

---

[3]W. T. Stace, "Mysticism and Human Reason," *University of Arizona Bulletin Series* 26 (1955): 19.

[4]Ibid., p. 20.

[5]John Baillie, *The Idea of Revelation in Recent Thought* (New York: Columbia University Press, 1956), p. 29.

[6]William Temple, *Nature, Man and God* (New York: St. Martin's Press, 1934), pp. 316, 322.

Temple marks a dramatic break with a major tradition of historic Christianity, a tradition that affirmed both an intelligible revelation from God and the divinely given human ability to know the transcendent God through the medium of true propositions. But this former confidence about God's ability to communicate information and the God-given human ability to receive that information has been shaken. The possibility of human knowledge about God has been denied on at least three grounds. (1) Some have precluded knowledge about God on the basis of particular theories about *the nature of human knowledge.* (2) Others have been led to agnosticism because of their view of *the nature of God.* For example, some have so exaggerated the divine transcendence that the Wholly Other God of whom they speak could not possibly be an object of human knowledge. (3) Still others have affirmed the impossibility of knowledge about God because of theories about *the nature of human language.* They regard human language as incapable of serving as an adequate carrier of information about God.

One of the fundamental postulates of contemporary nonevangelical theory, then, is the claim that God cannot reveal truth to us. And even if God could speak, humans are considered incapable of understanding whatever God might be attempting to say. The human relationship to God must, therefore, be understood according to a model other than that of receiving information or truth. It must be understood as an inward personal experience with God. No evangelical theologian denies the importance of a human encounter with the living God; but it is appropriate to question the consequences of divorcing the experience of God from cognitive knowledge about God.

The purpose of this book is to challenge the major forms of Christian agnosticism and offer an alternative theory that makes human knowledge about God possible. The theory is not new. In fact, it is a return to the classical Logos doctrine that played such a prominent role in the thinking of many early Christian writers. The view gained such influence in Christian thought that, centuries after it ceased to be discussed explicitly, it continued to control theological thinking about divine revelation and human capacity to know God. This is certainly evident in the writings of St. Augustine, who seldom mentions the Logos doctrine as such but whose entire approach to a Christian theory of knowledge is grounded on the doctrine.

In a sense, all of the issues to be discussed in this book reduce to one fundamental question: Can the human logos know the logos of God? In other words, is there a relationship between the human mind and the divine mind that is sufficient to ground the communication of truth from God to humans? There was no doubt in Christian thought that such a relationship exists and that such knowledge is possible until alien theories of knowledge gained ascendancy in the decades after Hume and Kant. This book is a counterattack to the prevailing agnosticism of contemporary Christian theology. Like Carl F. H. Henry, we wish to emphasize that

> the God of the Bible is a rational God; that the divine Logos is central to the Godhead and is the agent in creation and redemption; that man was made in the divine image for intelligible communion with God; that God communicates his purposes and truths about himself in the biblical revelation; that the Holy Spirit uses truth as a means of persuasion and conviction; and that Christian experience includes not simply a surrender of the will but a rational assent to the truth of God.[7]

There is nothing in the nature of the divine transcendence that precludes the possibility of our knowing the mind of God. There is nothing irrational or illogical about the content of divine revelation. The Christian God is not the Unknown God of ancient Athens or modern Marburg. He is a God who created men and women as creatures capable of knowing His mind and will and who has made information about His mind and will available in revealed truths.

When modern theologians claim that the word of God and the human mind are incompatible, they advance a position for which the world still awaits adequate argumentation. The case for this position has not yet been made. It has been advanced on the basis of questionable premises, and drastic oversimplifications, misunderstandings, or misrepresentations of the evangelical position. The fact that this agnosticism has been proposed by many who thought they were doing Christianity a favor is essentially irrelevant. Many proponents of the view did indeed believe that they were making a defense of Christianity easier by

---

[7]Carl F. H. Henry, "Reply to the God-Is-Dead Mavericks," *Christianity Today* 10 (May 27, 1966), p. 894.

rejecting knowledge in order to make room for faith. Theologians like Brunner, Tillich, and Bultmann sincerely believed their view would make it easier for moderns to enter into a genuine relationship with God. Good intentions do not guarantee sound theology. The inevitable implications of this position are destructive of historic Christianity.

Chapter 1

Hume's Gap: The Divorce of Faith and Knowledge

The writings of David Hume (1711–1776), like those of Immanuel Kant, are a watershed in the history of philosophy and theology. Hume's ideas on religion are found primarily in the last three sections of his *Enquiry Concerning Human Understanding* (section X being his famous essay on miracles), his classic *Dialogues Concerning Natural Religion*, and in several shorter essays on subjects such as suicide, immortality, and the natural history of religion.[1] Urged by several friends (including some clergymen), Hume agreed to delay publication of the *Dialogues* until after his death. They contain a profound and (as it turned out) influential analysis of the empirical arguments for God's existence, especially the argument from design. Among students of Hume's thought, they are also notorious for their ambiguity regarding Hume's final position.[2]

Much of Hume's notoriety among Christians results from a less

---

[1]Hume's *Enquiry* and *Dialogues* are readily available in a variety of editions. The other writings can be found in *The Philosophical Works of David Hume*, ed. T. H. Green and T. H. Grose, 4 vols., first published in London in 1874–1875.

[2]See the commentary by Nelson Pike in his edition of Hume's *Dialogues Concerning Natural Religion* (Indianapolis: Bobbs-Merrill, 1970). Other helpful studies of Hume's views about religion include John Charles Anderson Gaskin, *Hume's Philosophy of Religion* (New York: Barnes and Noble, 1978); Norman Kemp Smith, *The Philosophy of David Hume* (London: Macmillan, 1949); E. C. Mossner, *The Life of David Hume* (Oxford: Clarendon Press, 1970); Keith Yandell, "Hume's Philosophy of Religious Belief," (1979): 94–109; Keith Yandell, "Hume on Religious Belief," in *Hume: A Revaluation*, ed. D. W. Livingston and J. T. King (New York: Fordham University Press, 1976); and James Noxon, "Hume's Agnosticism," *Philosophical Review* 73 (1964): 248–261. Several helpful articles appear in the collection, *McGill Hume Studies*, edited by Norton, Capaldi, and Robison (San Diego: Austin Hill Press, 1979).

than careful reading of his works. Hume is commonly believed to have attacked the foundations of Christianity, such as the existence of God, personal survival after death, and miracles. It is true that Hume's personal beliefs about many Christian doctrines did not mirror the orthodox Calvinism that surrounded him in his early youth. What Hume intended in his writings is often quite removed from what his interpreters have thought.

Hume's major threat to Christianity comes not from the theories for which he gained notoriety,[3] but rather from his espousal of a notion that has, in fact, become widely held in Christendom. Before Hume's position on that subject is discussed, some general remarks about the philosophical background of Hume's teaching may be helpful.

There are three common misconceptions about Hume's philosophy. The first: Hume denied the reality of causal relations, that there is ever a necessary connection between that prior event we call a cause and the subsequent event we call its effect. Two, that Hume rejected the existence of what philosophers call the external world; that is, that he doubted the existence of a real world outside of his mind. Hume, it is claimed, was a solipsist and a sceptic. Three, that Hume doubted the existence of what philosophers call the self, that is, the real I, the foundation of a person's identity through time. These three erroneous claims make up what might be called the philosophical package. What led to their promulgation has a bearing on one of Hume's key doctrines and through that doctrine is linked to the central concern of this chapter.

The philosophical package came to be attributed to Hume because of the writings of two of his fellow Scotsmen, Thomas Reid and James Beattie,[4] who became famous for their defense of common sense against the supposed scepticism of Hume. Reid and Beattie believed that Hume had simply borrowed some premises from the empiricism of two earlier British philosophers, John Locke and George Berkeley, and had extended those doctrines to their logical but bitter end, namely, total scepticism about God, the world, and the self.

---

[3] That is, his views about the theistic arguments, miracles, and survival after death.

[4] Beattie's major work in this area was his *Essay on the Nature and Immutability of Truth*, first published in Edinburgh in 1770. Thomas Reid is, by far, the more significant philosopher of the two. In fact, his own position has received renewed attention in recent years. Worth consulting is his *Essays on the Intellectual Powers of Man*, first published in 1786, reprinted several times.

But Hume's entire enterprise was quite different from what Reid and Beattie envisaged. According to Hume, everyone holds to a number of pivotal beliefs around which most other beliefs, individual actions, and social institutions turn. These pivotal beliefs include the reality of causal relations (that some things can and do cause changes in other things), the reality of the external world (that the existence of the world does not depend upon its being perceived), and the continuing existence of the knowing self. Hume had no quarrel with these beliefs; it would be fundamentally foolish he held, to doubt them. What most concerned Hume was how these beliefs come to be "known." Hume showed that neither reason nor experience is sufficient to ground a knowledge of these matters. But there simply is no other way for them to be known. Therefore, if these pivotal beliefs cannot be known by reason and experience, they cannot be known at all.

It was at this point that Reid and Beattie made one of their mistakes. They jumped to the conclusion that Hume was actually denying these pivotal beliefs. They were wrong. Hume was denying that there is any sense in which we can be said to *know* these things. But this is a far cry from saying that we should *doubt* them. That would be the height of folly. Obviously, we must continue to believe them since the consequences of not believing are too absurd to contemplate. And no one has to force or persuade us to believe them; believing them is the *natural* thing to do. With this last observation we begin to approach Hume's basic point: Hume tried to show that most of our pivotal beliefs about reality are matters that human reason is powerless to prove or support.

HUME'S GAP

Hume was really doing two things. First, he was attacking the supremacy of human reason, one of the cardinal tenets of the Enlightenment, by seeking to show that human reason has definite limits. All who attempt to extend reason beyond its limits become involved in absurdities and contradictions and become prone to the disease of scepticism.[5] Philosophers have been entirely too optimistic in assessing the

---

[5]As I show in chapter 2, this conviction was also a fundamental thesis of Kant. The claim that there are more similarities between Hume and Kant than meet the eye is argued by Lewis White Beck in his article, "A Prussian Hume and a Scottish Kant," in *McGill Hume Studies*, pp. 63–78.

claims of human reason, Hume believed. Most of the important things we think we know are not known at all. That is, they have not been arrived at on the basis of reasoning and they are not supported by experience. Hume's second point was that these pivotal beliefs rest on something other than reason and experience, namely, on instinct, habit, and custom. Some nonrational inner force compels us to accept these pivotal beliefs. In his writings on ethics also, Hume argued that moral judgments rest not on reason but on nonrational human nature. In ethics, as in metaphysics and religion, human reason is and ought to be the slave of human passions, that is, our nonrational nature.[6] This is tantamount to the claim that we cannot have *knowledge* about the transcendent. This axiom is the foundation of what I call "Hume's Gap."

If Hume was a sceptic, then, he was not one in James Beattie's sense of the word. Hume did not doubt the existence of the world. As Hume saw it, this kind of scepticism is absurd because it contradicts common sense and violates our natural instinct to believe (against all reasoning) in certain propositions.[7] Nature, instinct, and common sense all lead us to believe in an external world. According to Hume, we should ignore the arguments of the rationalists and trust our instincts. He believed that investigation ought to be limited to areas, such as mathematics, where knowledge is possible. Speculative knowledge-claims about certain topics in metaphysics, theology, and ethics should be avoided;[8] such matters should be accepted on the basis of *faith*, not knowledge.

Hume's religious beliefs are, for the most part, an extension of the position just outlined. But some blatant distortions of his religious posi-

---

[6]Hume's well-known statement about reason being the slave of the passions appears in his *Treatise of Human Nature*, II, iii.

[7]The possibility that Hume's position was essentially the same as that advanced by the Scottish Common Sense philosophers Beattie and Reid is examined by David Fate Norton in his essay, "Hume and His Scottish Critics," in *McGill Hume Studies*, pp. 309–24.

[8]This is what Hume really meant in the famous conclusion to his *Enquiry Concerning Human Understanding*: "When we run over libraries, persuaded of these principles, what havoc must we make? If we take in our hand any volume; of divinity or school metaphysics, for instance; let us ask, *Does it contain any abstract reasoning concerning quantity or number?* No. *Does it contain any experimental reasoning concerning matter of fact and existence?* No. Commit it then to the flames: for it can contain nothing but sophistry and illusion."

tion should be rejected. It is sometimes thought that Hume was an atheist, that he attempted to prove God does not exist, and that he argued that miracles are impossible. To be sure, Hume was not a Christian in the New Testament sense of the word. He did not believe in miracles (which is, however, something quite different from trying to prove them impossible). He did not personally believe in special revelation or immortality or religious duties like prayer. But he was not an atheist; he did not attempt to prove the nonexistence of God. And he certainly never argued that miracles are impossible. (This claim will surprise some readers. Hume's famous attack on miracles really amounts to the assertion that no one could ever *reasonably* believe that a miracle had occurred.)

Hume believed in the existence of a divine mind that was in some unknown way responsible for the order of the universe.[9] Hume was both shocked and amused by the dogmatic atheism of the French *philosophes*. Their mistake was the same as that of the orthodox Calvinists: each thought they could obtain knowledge about the transcendent; but unlike the Calvinists, the *philosophes* thought this knowledge would justify their conclusion that a transcendent being did *not* exist.

It would have been inconsistent for Hume to attempt to disprove God's existence. His point was that we cannot have any knowledge about God. But it is entirely natural to have faith that God exists. In fact, the same nature that compels us to hold the pivotal beliefs mentioned earlier leads us to believe in the existence of God.

But nature does not compel us to go beyond this basic belief in God's existence and accept the theological claims added by orthodoxy. Those theological claims must be rejected because they go beyond the limits of human knowledge. To argue, as many Christians do, that reason can prove the existence of God,[10] or that reason can infer many of the divine attributes from features of the world, and that the Christian religion (or any religion, for that matter) is supported by miraculous

---

[9]Consider the following quote from Hume's *Natural History of Religion* (in *The Philosophical Works of David Hume*, 4, 309): "The whole frame of nature bespeaks an intelligent author; and no rational enquirer can, after serious reflection, suspend his belief a moment with regard to the primary principles of genuine. Theism and Religion." In this connection, section XII of the *Dialogues* should be studied. Student's of Hume's thought know how difficult it is to reconcile everything Hume says in this work. Worth consulting are Nelson Pike's notes to his edition of the *Dialogues*.

[10]Obviously, many Christians disagree with this claim.

events, is to exceed the bounds of human knowledge. These claims, according to Hume, must be rejected, as must the many assertions that Christians make about God in their creeds, items allegedly derived from special revelation. Without doubt, some Christians have overestimated the ability of human reason with respect to "proofs" about God's existence. I have no desire to attempt any defense of that use of reason. More serious, however, is Hume's denial of the possibility of *any* knowledge about God in general and the possibility of revealed knowledge in particular.

To summarize, Hume's goal in his discussions of religion was the same as his objective in philosophy: he wished to show that reason is powerless to convert anyone to the claims of faith. "To be a philosophical sceptic," he wrote, "is the first and most essential step towards being a sound believing Christian."[11] Hume's own preference seems to have been for a nonrational faith in a god unsupported by reason, revelation, miracles, or evidence of any kind.

With this background, the nature of what I earlier referred to as Hume's Gap can now be identified. Hume's Gap is the rejection of the possibility of a rational knowledge of God and objective religious truth. Hume grounded man's belief in God in man's nonrational nature. Hume was a precursor of those philosophers and theologians who insist that religious faith must be divorced from knowledge and who believe that the impossibility of knowledge about God will in some way enhance faith. Like Kant, Hume was engaged in denying knowledge in order to make room for faith. To both Hume and Kant, knowledge and faith have nothing in common. The arrogance of rational religion must be destroyed so that faith (a nonrational faith, that is) can assume its proper place as the only legitimate ground of religion.

Hume's Gap appears prominently in the thought of a great many modern thinkers. The contemporary eclipse of God can be seen in Sartre's "silence of God," in Heidegger's "absence of God," in Jasper's "concealment of God," in Bultmann's "hiddenness of God," in Tillich's "non-being of God," and finally in radical theology's assertion of

---

[11]The quotation comes from the conclusion to Section 12 of Hume's *Dialogues Concerning Natural Religion.* J. G. Hamann believed that Hume's scepticism could be a godsend for Christianity. He translated Hume's *Dialogues* into German, hoping it would lead rationalists like Immanuel Kant to see the light.

"the death of God." St. Paul's sermon to the philosophers on Mars Hill (Acts 17) concerning worship of the Unknown God is all too relevant to the contemporary theological scene. Nonevangelical theology since Hume is a chronicle of futile attempts to retain respectability for religious faith while denying religion any right to revealed truth. In Paul Tillich's version of Hume's thesis, all that is left of Christianity is a "religion" that is neither objective, rational, miraculous, supernatural, nor even personal. Apparently, about the only thing nonevangelical thinkers can agree about is that God has not spoken and, indeed, cannot speak. Neo-orthodox theology, because of its outspoken denial of cognitive revelation, is not an exception.

While contemporary non-Evangelicals have virtually reduced faith to "courageous ignorance,"[12] Evangelicals have hardly been faithful in defending God's objective communication of truth. Hume's Gap has infected modern orthodoxy to the extent that many Evangelicals are either ignoring or de-emphasizing the cognitive dimension of divine revelation.

A new anti-intellectualism threatens contemporary Evangelicalism. It is evident in much evangelical disregard for the revealed truth of God and in the effort by some Evangelicals to substitute other concerns for that truth. Christian anti-intellectualism may be manifested in a variety of ways: in a contempt for creeds, in a search for God through the emotions, in a dependence upon some kind of mystical experience. Hume would be comfortable in many contemporary churches for he would not hear the truth of God proclaimed and defended. He would hear stories and testimonies that appeal to the emotions.[13] Hume might even be welcomed as a professor in some evangelical theological seminaries. He would find acceptance among the religious irrationalists of the day who hold that the quotient of faith increases as its rational content decreases.

The most obvious consequence of Hume's Gap is a minimal theism. Once Hume's stance is adopted, New Testament Christianity, with its proclamation of a divine Christ whose death and resurrection

---

[12]Carl F. H. Henry, "Justification by Ignorance: A Neo-Protestant Motif?" *Journal of the Evangelical Theological Society* 13 (1970): 13.

[13]I am not impugning the value of the emotions and religious experience in the quest for religious truth. My target is those who set these up as an *alternative* to reason and insist that we must not rationally reflect on our experiences and emotions.

secured redemption from sin and gave hope beyond the grave, must be replaced with a religion that talks about how good it feels to have an experience with a god about whom nothing definite can be known.

The threat to Christianity today from the legacy of David Hume is not a full-fledged frontal assault upon Christian theism, with all the troops advancing in full light of day. That kind of attack would fail because it would arouse Christians to a rational defense of their faith. David Hume's legacy is more insidious. It undermines the faith not by denying it but by directing our attention away from the importance of its knowledge-claims and its truth-content.

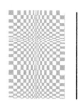 # Theological Agnosticism from Kant to Ritschl

At the end of the last chapter, we got slightly ahead of our story. But this was necessary in order to indicate the extent to which the contemporary agnosticism within Christian thought images what I have called Hume's Gap. This done, we can now turn to the second thinker of the eighteenth century whose system has encouraged scepticism about the possibility of knowledge about God. That thinker is the German philosopher, Immanuel Kant (1724–1804), whose system is well-known for its complexity.

Kant readily acknowledged his debt to Hume. He wrote, "I openly confess my recollection of David Hume was the very thing which many years ago first interrupted my dogmatic slumber and gave my investigations in the field of speculative philosophy a quite new direction."[1] Kant thought that Hume's work contained a spark which, if fanned, could ignite a revolution in philosophy. Kant ventured to suggest that perhaps even Hume himself did not fully see the implications of his attack on metaphysics. Kant was scornful of the misinterpretations of Hume in the writings of Reid and Beattie:

> It is positively painful to see how utterly his opponents, Reid, Oswald, Beattie, and lastly Priestley, missed the point of the problem; for while they were ever taking for granted

---

[1]Immanuel Kant, *Prolegomena to Any Future Metaphysics* (New York: Liberal Arts Press, 1950), p. 8. Kant's relation to the thought of Hume is a subject of much controversy. A good overview of this debate (along with suggestions of the position I take) can be found in Lewis White Beck's "A Prussian Hume and a Scottish Kant," in *McGill Hume Studies*.

that which he doubted, and demonstrating with zeal and often with impudence that which he never thought of doubting, they so misconstrued his valuable suggestion that everything remained in its old condition, as if nothing had happened.[2]

Kant regarded his own system as a veritable Copernican revolution in philosophy. Just as Copernicus had revolutionized the model of the solar system by placing the sun instead of the earth at its center, so Kant believed his system would produce a similar upheaval in philosophy. Philosophers prior to Kant (or so Kant claimed) had assumed that human knowledge is possible only as the mind is adapted to the world. Kant reversed this order.[3] Instead of the mind adapting to the supposed objects of its knowledge, all objects are instead adapted to the knowing mind. The universal and necessary features of reality are known to be features of reality by virtue of their *first* being characteristics of the human mind which seeks to know. The rationality (that is, the universality and necessity) that human beings find in nature is there precisely because the human mind puts it there.

Kant sought to go beyond both rationalism and empiricism by making human knowledge a composite of two factors, form and content. The content is given by sense experience. In fact, all human knowledge begins with sense experience. But, "although all our knowledge begins with experience, it does not follow that it arises from experience."[4] What Kant means is that while sense experience is necessary for human knowledge in the sense that no one would have any knowledge without it, sense experience is not a sufficient condition for knowledge. Something else (a form or structure) must be added to the content supplied by the senses. Unless the content is given form or structure by the human mind, knowledge would be unattainable. As Kant put it, concepts (the form supplied by the human understanding) without per-

---

[2]*Prolegomena*, p. 60.

[3]In Kant's words, "Hitherto it has been assumed that all our knowledge must conform to objects. But all attempts to extend our knowledge of objects by establishing something in regard to them *a priori*, by means of concepts, have, on this assumption, ended in failure. We must therefore make trial whether we may not have more success in the tasks of metaphysics, if we suppose that objects must conform to our knowledge." Kant, Introduction to the 2nd edition of *The Critique of Pure Reason*, Norman Kemp Smith translation (New York: St. Martin's Press, 1965).

[4]Ibid.

cepts (the content supplied by the senses) are empty; percepts without concepts are blind. Human knowledge, then, has two necessary conditions: the form supplied by the mind and the content supplied by the senses. But neither condition is sufficient by itself to produce knowledge.

Kant taught that the form or structure that the human understanding supplies to knowledge exists in the form of categories or innate aptitudes for knowing. Since all human knowledge must be mediated by these categories, men cannot *know* anything that is not so mediated. The unfortunate consequence of this claim, however, was a radical disjunction between the world as it appears to us (the world modified by the categories of our understanding) and the world as it really is. According to Kant, human knowledge never brings us into contact with the real world, what he called the *noumenal world.* All we ever know is the *phenomenal world,* the world as it appears to us after it has been modified by the categories of our understanding. Since our knowledge is always perceptually modified by the a priori* categories of the mind, the real world *(noumena)* is not only unknown but unknowable.

Hume had his Gap; Kant had his Wall. Kant's system had the effect of erecting a wall between the world as it appears to us and the world as it really is. Human knowledge is restricted to the phenomenal world, the world of appearance, the world shaped by the structure of the knowing mind. Knowledge of any reality beyond the Wall, which includes the world of things in themselves, is forever unattainable. Human reason cannot penetrate the secrets of ultimate reality. Answers to the most basic questions of theology and metaphysics lie beyond the boundaries of human knowledge. Since God is not a subject of experience and since the human categories cannot be extended to transcendent reality, Kant's God is both unknown and unknowable. Whenever human reason attempts to penetrate beyond Kant's Wall, either in a search for knowledge about God or in a quest for answers to ultimate questions, it becomes involved in antinomies or contradictions.

Ironically, Kant thought his agnosticism with respect to God was an aid to Christian faith. Kant actually thought he was serving the interests of the Christian religion. He wrote that he had "found it

---

*In Kant's thought, this phrase refers to that which is independent of sense experience.

necessary to deny *knowledge*, in order to make room for faith."[5] They had come to their destination by different routes, but both Hume and Kant arrived at very nearly the same point. For both Hume and Kant, faith and knowledge have nothing in common. Every time human reason attempts to leap across Hume's Gap or tries to break through Kant's Wall separating the phenomenal and noumenal worlds (as speculative metaphysics and theology seek to do), reason becomes bogged down in contradictions. Human reason cannot penetrate the secrets of ultimate reality. The most basic questions of metaphysics and theology are questions to which human reason can find no answers, not even from God. Hume's Gap and Kant's Wall represent the limits beyond which human reason cannot go;[6] they imply, among other things, that human knowledge about God is an unattainable goal.

In Kant's system of thought, God *does* have a role to play.[7] Even though God was one of the unknowables, Kant managed to slip Him in through the back door as a necessary postulate required to salvage morality. For Kant, the existence of God was entirely a matter of faith, to which Kant gave a distinctively practical twist. The Christian should abandon any knowledge-claims about the transcendent and take refuge in a faith grounded not in theoretical but on moral and practical considerations.[7]

FRIEDRICH SCHLEIERMACHER

As the eighteenth century passed into the nineteenth, Kant's rejection of the possibility of cognitive knowledge of God was taken up by a succession of thinkers including Friedrich Schleiermacher (1768–1834) and Albrecht Ritschl (1822–1889), both of whom became major sources of Protestant liberalism. Schleiermacher's first important book, *On Religion: Addresses in Response to its Cultured Critics*, appeared in 1799. Schleiermacher thought of his own work as a reaction against Kant's reduction of religion to an ethical exercise of the will. But despite

---

[5] Ibid., p. 29.

[6] There is an important difference between Hume and Kant on this point. While Hume regarded faith as nonrational because it was based on custom or instinct, Kant believed that faith could be grounded in *practical* reason.

[7] Not all Evangelicals share my negative assessment of the implications of Kant's position. For an alternate view, see C. Stephen Evans, *Subjectivity and Religious Belief* (Washington, D.C.: Christian University Press, 1978).

his protests against Kant, Schleiermacher's position in the end became an extension of Kant's theological agnosticism.

Distinguishing between the kernel and the husk of religion, Schleiermacher suggested that many of the cultured despisers of religion in his day were in fact offended by nonessential elements of Christianity. This dispensable husk of religion, in his view, included the metaphysical theories and theological doctrines that so many unbelieving intellectuals found incredible. He wrote:

> For what are these doctrinal structures, these systems of theology, these theories about the origin and end of the world, these analyses concerning the nature of an incomprehensible being? Here everything elapses into callous argumentation. Here even the sublimest subjects are made pawns of controversy between competing schools of thought. Now surely . . . this is not the character of religion. If, therefore, you have paid attention only to these religious dogmas and opinions, you do not yet know religion itself at all, and religion is not what you are objecting to. Why haven't you gone deeper to find the kernel lying inside these outer layers?[8]

Schleiermacher's *On Religion* went on to reject two erroneous approaches to religion. On the one hand, he attacked those who thought of religion primarily as a way of thinking or knowing something. Among those who followed this way were the orthodox who stressed the importance of right thinking and correct doctrine. On the other hand, Schleiermacher criticized those who, like Kant, viewed religion primarily as a way of living or doing, as a kind of conduct or character. For Schleiermacher, religion must not be confused either with knowing or with doing. For him, true religion is found in feeling.[9] Schleiermacher was convinced that only someone who has known and studied the human experience in moments of religious ecstasy can know what

---

[8]Friedrich Schleiermacher, *On Religion: Addresses in Response to Its Cultured Critics* (Richmond, Virginia: John Knox Press, 1969), p. 55.

[9]"Look especially at those extraordinary moments when a person's spirit is so caught up in the highest reaches of piety that all other activities known to you are restrained, almost supplanted by it—moments in which one's feeling is wholly absorbed in an immediate sense of the infinite and eternal and of its fellowship with the soul" (Ibid., pp. 55–56).

religion really is and can distinguish religion from its accidental, non-essential outward manifestations. Since it is a mistake to think of religion primarily in terms of thinking or willing, "Faith must be something quite different from a mishmash of opinions about God and the world [the theoretical approach] or a collocation of commands for one life or two [the practical way of Kant]. Piety must be something more than the craving after this hodgepodge of metaphysical and moral crumbs, something more than a way of stirring them up."[10] True religion must renounce such metaphysical and pratical concerns. Piety does not increase in proportion to an increase of knowledge. In fact, religion should not be thought of in terms of knowledge. The most important dimension of the religious life in Schleiermacher's account is neither knowing nor acting, but feeling.

Schleiermacher's two volume work *The Christian Faith* (published 1821–1822) reinterpreted all of Christian theology in terms of this emphasis on religious feeling. Central to his later work was the conviction that the essence of religion is to be found in a human being's *feeling* of absolute dependence. "The common element in all howsoever diverse expressions of piety . . . is this: the consciousness of being absolutely dependent, or, which is the same thing, of being in relation with God."[11] Later in the same book he wrote, "God-consciousness is always . . . the feeling of absolute dependence."[12]

Schleiermacher's view reduces to the position that God is unknowable to the human intellect. Instead of looking for God in nature or in the Bible or in human reason, we should look within. God is to be found in a special kind of feeling, the feeling of absolute dependence. Some recent defenders of Schleiermacher have complained about the tendency of many interpreters to make the feeling about which he wrote too much a matter of emotion and too little a matter of thought.[13]

---

[10]Ibid., p. 73.

[11]Friedrich Schleiermacher, *The Christian Faith*, tr. from second German edition, ed. H. R. Mackintosh and J. S. Steward (Edinburgh: T. & T. Clark, 1928), p. 12.

[12]Ibid., p. 260.

[13]See, for example, Paul Tillich, *Dynamics of Faith* (New York: Harper and Row, 1957), pp. 38–39. See also C. W. Christian, *Friedrich Schleiermacher* (Waco, Texas: Word, 1979). For a bibliography of older writings about Schleiermacher, consult Richard B. Brandt, *The Philosophy of Schleiermacher* (New York: Harper and Bros., 1941). An interesting source on Schleiermacher that is often overlooked is Karl Barth's "Concluding Unscientific Postscript on Schleiermacher," *Studies in Religion* 7 (1978): 117–135. The

Whether later interpreters, liberal or conservative, understood Schleier-macher correctly or not, he came to be regarded as the fountainhead of one dominant form of liberalism, namely, the view that it doesn't matter what a person believers, it is what he *feels* that is important. Liberals who shared this view and regarded Schleiermacher as its proximate source, descended on the pulpits of many establishment churches in America like a plague of locusts. Schleiermacher's greatest influence, which continued at least through the 1960's, resulted from the fact that people thought he meant to exclude any cognitive content from the Christian faith. It is ironic that although Schleiermacher thought he was offering the world an alternative to Kant's theory of religion, Schleiermacher's legacy to Protestant theology came to be regarded as an extension of Kant's disjunction between religion and theoretical knowledge.

It is clear that Schleiermacher thought it wrong to regard revelation as any kind of human discovery. Whatever revelation is, it is not some-thing "excogitated in thought by one man and so learned by others."[14] As H. D. McDonald explains, revelation for Schleiermacher "is not an inbreaking of God, but an upsurging of divine humanity."[15] Schleier-macher insisted that God can never be known as He is in Himself. We can only know God as God-in-relation-to-humans. Because of his exaggerated emphasis on divine immanence, Schleiermacher con-cluded that God is too close to contemplate with any objectivity. In fact, he wrote, "All attributes which we ascribe to God are to be taken as denoting not something special in God, but only something special in the manner in which the feeling of absolute dependence is to be related to him."[16] The divine attributes, then, are not objective properties of God; they are merely reflections of human feelings.

Schleiermacher went on to reinterpret most of the major doctrines of Christianity in terms of the feeling of ultimate dependence that he regarded as the essence of the Christian faith. Apparently, Schleier-macher's God was anything which can produce the feeling of absolute

---

article, originally published in German in 1968, reviews the several changes in Barth's attitude toward Schleiermacher.

[14]Schleiermacher, *The Christian Faith*, p. 50.

[15]H. D. McDonald, *Ideas of Revelation, An Historical Study:* A.D. 1700–A.D. 1860 (Grand Rapids: Baker, 1959), p. 169.

[16]*Christian Faith*, p. 194.

dependence. For him, religion is not knowing something or doing something (compare Ritschl) but *feeling* something. The major emphases mentioned in our earlier discussions of Hume's Gap and Kant's Wall can be clearly seen in Schleiermacher's system. Schleiermacher's God is unknowable by the human mind; He can only be felt in the unique experience of absolute dependence.

ALBRECHT RITSCHL

The second major source of Protestant liberalism was the work of Albrecht Ritschl.[17] Ritschl protested loudly against Schleiermacher's religious subjectivism and professed to seek a ground for Christian faith that would be more objective and less relativistic than Schleiermacher's. He claimed to find this ground in the objectivity provided by history. Unfortunately, Ritschl's concern for objectivity did not take him very far; for his search within history for objective information about Jesus was selectively controlled by two presuppositions he borrowed from Kant.

The first was that, like Kant, Ritschl excluded metaphysics from theology. Just as Kant had consigned God and metaphysical questions to the unknowable world of *noumena*, Ritschl rejected speculative theism as irrelevant. Ritschl consequently condemned all ecclesiastical dogma as illegitimate offspring of metaphysics and speculative theology. This meant that the Jesus whom Ritschl "found" in history was a Jesus conveniently matched to his own liberal presuppositions. Questions about the deity of Jesus, the relationship between his human and divine natures, and his relationship to God the Father had no place in the theology of Ritschl.

The second controlling assumption Ritschl borrowed from Kant was the conviction that what ultimately counted in religion was ethics. While Kant had kicked God out the front door (theory), he sneaked Him in the back door (ethics). Religion should be concerned with morality, not theoretical concerns. The important thing about religion is its practical effect on the life of believers, not what they know of a

---

[17]Background on Ritschl can be gleaned from a number of sources including the following: James Richmond, *Ritschl: A Reappraisal* (London: Collins, 1978); James Orr, *The Ritschlian Theology and the Evangelical Faith* (New York: Thomas Whittaker, 1898); James Orr, *Ritschlianism* (London, 1903); R. Mackintosh, *Albrecht Ritschl and His School* (London, 1915).

body of propositions. This Kantian emphasis appeared in Ritschl's system in the form of a distinction between two kinds of judgment: judgments of value and theoretical judgments. While theoretical judgments are objective and analyzable, value judgments are not. While both kinds of judgment are proper in their place, theoretical judgments are out of place in religious inquiry. Ritschl's distinction, of course, is a subtle reintroduction of Kant's Wall, and the Christian who seeks to attain theoretical truth about religion must bump up against it. The only kind of knowledge attainable in religion is dependent on value judgments. It is wrong, Ritschl wrote, to "strive after a purely theoretical or 'disinterested' knowledge of God as an indispensable preliminary to the knowledge of faith. To be sure, people say that we must first know the nature of God and Christ ere we can ascertain their value for us. But Luther's insight perceived the incorrectness of such a view. The truth rather is that we know the nature of God and Christ only *in* their value for us."[18]

Ritschl, like Kant, turns out to be an antimetaphysical moralist who rejects theological speculation about such traditional concerns as Christology and soteriology. Theoretical judgments in religion should be abandoned in favor of an emphasis on practical moral issues. And when Ritschl finished sifting his "objective data" of history through this sieve of Kantian presuppositions, not surprisingly the historical Jesus he discovered turns out to be an advocate of his own brand of Protestant liberalism. According to Ritschl, the only sure information about Jesus is his moral teaching.

Ritschl's claim that "we know the nature of God and Christ only *in* their value for us" pounds the final nail into the coffin of his alleged objectivism. While Ritschl began by rejecting Schleiermacher's position as too subjectivistic, he ended up advocating a subjectivism of his own. The only real knowledge human beings can have of God is in the effects God has upon us. Ritschl's objectivism, like the Cheshire cat, has performed an amazing disappearing act. In spite of all Ritschl's professed concern about an objective basis for faith in history, he ends up founding the Christian religion on the shifting sands of a person's religious consciousness.

---

[18]Albrecht Ritschl, *The Christian Doctrine of Justification and Reconciliation*, tr. H. R. Mackintosh and A. A. Macaulay, 3 vols. (Edinburgh: T & T. Clark, 1900), 3:212.

I am not suggesting that religious emotion and moral values are unimportant concerns of the Christian faith. Religious life is supposed to make an impact on the emotions and values of the believer. But Schleiermacher and Ritschl did Christianity a disservice by cutting the affective and moral dimensions of Christian experience off from the kinds of objective and rational moorings that faith must have. Thus do Kant's Wall and Hume's Gap reappear in the thought of both Schleiermacher and Ritschl. For Schleiermacher, they assume the form of the disjunction between knowledge and feeling. For Ritschl, they become the disjunction between knowledge and value, between knowing and doing, between theory and practice.[19]

---

[19]Many people think that Søren Kierkegaard epitomized the subjectivism and irrationalism that has come to characterize so much of contemporary theology. Certainly this was the way Karl Barth read Kierkegaard in the 1920's. According to this interpretation of Kierkegaard, the more unreasonable Christianity is, the better. Moreover, it is frequently thought that Kierkegaard rejected any place for objectively revealed truth in religion because such objectivity would impede the passionate subjectivity that is so essential to genuine faith. This way of interpreting Kierkegaard has been effectively critiqued by C. Stephen Evans in two recent articles: "Kierkegaard on Subjective Truth: Is God an Ethical Fiction?", *International Journal for Philosophy of Religion* VII (1976): 288ff. and "Kierkegaard's Attack on Apologetics," *Christian Scholars' Review* (1981): 322ff. According to Evans, Kierkegaard is easy to misunderstand because he cared so passionately about his subject and frequently wrote with such emotion that he lapsed into careless, imprecise, or exaggerated statements. In Evans' view, Kierkegaard never denied the relevance of objective truth for the Christian faith, although his sometimes intemperate language or unclear intentions may give that impression. In fact, Evans insists, Kierkegaard's position makes no sense at all unless he also held to the possibility and relevance of objective and propositional revealed truth. Instead of holding that right belief is not important, Kierkegaard's position was that in the arena of ethical and religious choice, one's beliefs should be permitted to transform his existence.

Chapter 3

The Assault on Propositional Revelation

I have suggested that the theological scepticism that pervades contemporary Christian thought is a convergence of theories about the nature of human knowledge, the nature of God, and the nature of human language. Our brief study of Hume, Kant, Schleiermacher, and Ritschl helps us see the general direction taken by the first two of those streams of thought. Although Hume started the ball rolling, the two dominant forms of theological scepticism in the nineteenth century (Schleiermacher and Ritschl) largely followed the lead of Kant. As Protestant liberalism evolved in the first quarter of the twentieth century, its God increasingly came to resemble the pantheistic deity of Schleiermacher. Naturally, any cognitive communication from such a God is impossible. The liberal God could not speak because He was totally immanent in nature; He lacked personality.

The theological scepticism of the past sixty years, however, proceeds on the basis of a theory about the nature of God different from Schleiermacher's. When neo-orthodox theology first burst on the scene in the form of Karl Barth's commentary on the Epistle to the Romans, one of its more prominent concerns was the repudiation of Schleiermacher's immanence-theology. Barth went so far as to call the theology of Schleiermacher's disciples a "betrayal of Christ."[1] He rejected the immanence-theology of liberalism (which he himself had formerly held) in favor of a new emphasis on divine transcendence that he had

<hr />

[1]Karl Barth, *The Epistle to the Romans*, tr. Edwyn C. Hoskyns, 6th ed. (London: Oxford University Press, 1933 [1968]), p. 255.

learned from Kierkegaard, Luther, and the Scriptures. Unfortunately, this totally transcendent or wholly other God was no more able to communicate knowledge or truth than the immanent deity of Schleiermacher. The early Barth had denied that revelation is a communication of truth and viewed it only as personal divine-human encounter. And although much later Barth qualified this position considerably, it is still possible to trace a degree of ambivalence about the subject in his later writings.

The God of pantheistic liberalism could not speak because "He" was totally immanent; today, the reason most often given for God's inability to speak is His transcendence. This radical otherness of God means, among other things, that the human mind is incapable of comprehending the divine mind. Once this point is granted, it follows that the word of God can never be the communication of truth; divine revelation can never contain a cognitive content that can be apprehended by the human mind. This network of ideas accounts for what is perhaps the central phalanx in the contemporary assault on the knowability of God. It can be summed up in the statement that *no revelation is propositional*.

Advocates of this view usually begin by drawing a radical distinction between two senses of revelation, propositional revelation (the revelation of truth) and personal revelation. The distinction once granted becomes an exclusive disjunction, and proponents of the nonpropositional view of revelation then simply assert the impossibility of any cognitive knowledge[2] about God and insist that God reveals Himself, not through propositions, but through personal presence or encounter. According to this position, man does not require knowledge about God (propositional truth) as a precondition for a personal relationship with God. Revelation is exclusively an event in which God reveals Himself; it is *never* a disclosure of information about God or anything else.

The list of those who have held this noncognitive view of revelation reads like a Who's Who of contemporary theology. One of the earliest proponents of the position in the English-speaking world was the

---

[2]The phrase "cognitive knowledge" that we shall use occasionally is not redundant. It is offered in contrast to competing, more personal and noncognitive kinds of knowledge that play a prominent role in the writings of many modern theologians.

Archbishop of Canterbury, William Temple, who declared, "There is no such thing as revealed truth."[3]

On the European continent, Emil Brunner, following the early Karl Barth, maintained that "divine revelation is not a book or a doctrine; the Revelation is God Himself in His self-manifestation within history. Revelation is something that *happens*, the living history of God in his dealings with the human race."[4] Central to Brunner's doctrine of revelation was the claim that revelation is exclusively an event; it is God's breaking into history, into time in the person of Jesus Christ. For Brunner, revelation is not some doctrine *about* Jesus. It is Jesus Himself.

For Brunner, revelation is more than a self-manifestation on the part of God. It is personal correspondence. It is an address and a response in faith as the individual is confronted by God in Christ. It is an "I-Thou" relationship. Revelation is an encounter between two persons: God, in the person of Christ, and the individual.[5] It is not a one-sided affair. Revelation is an event which is transcendent, unique, absolute, personal, and unrepeatable. It cannot be proven since it has its own logic and rationality. In this revelatory encounter, there is no revealed truth. For Brunner, revelation "is not the communication of intellectual knowledge of a doctrine about God, but God's own personal Word."[6] God can only be known as subject, never as object. "The God of the Bible is . . . the unconditioned Subject. A 'subject,' in contradistinction to every kind of 'object,' is that which can be known absolutely only through self-communication."[7] The word *revelation*, then, in Brunner's view, "does not mean a supernaturally revealed doctrine. . . . In the Bible 'revelation' means God's mighty acts of man's Salvation."[8]

---

[3]William Temple, *Nature, Man and God*, p. 316.

[4]Emil Brunner, *Revelation and Reason*, tr. Olive Wyon (Philadelphia: Westminster, 1946), p. 8. Whatever Barth's view on this subject was during the 1920's, his thought clearly evolved to the point where he was willing to allow for the possibility of some divine communication of truth.

[5]Barth eventually found an encounter-model of revelation repugnant because it seemed to elevate the sinful human to the point where he or she made a contribution to the revelation that was as important as God's. Consequently, dropping all talk about revelation as encounter, Barth preferred to think of revelation purely in terms of God's speaking.

[6]Emil Brunner, *The Mediator*, tr. (Philadelphia: Westminster, 1947), p. 237. Copyright, W. L. Jenkins, used by permission.

[7]*Revelation and Reason*, p. 43.

[8]Ibid., p. 118.

Brunner found an interesting example of his position in the labels the RCA Victor Company once used on its phonograph records. Those labels depict a dog faithfully listening to an old Gramophone. The message on the label read, "His Master's Voice." Brunner thought this was an excellent illustration of the Bible's role in revelation. A Christian listening to the Bible cannot help but hear the scratches and distortions on the surface of the old record. But through the imperfections, he nonetheless hears *his* Master's voice. [9] Though the Bible itself is not the Word of God, nevertheless we can hear the Word of God through the Bible. "Just as the windowpanes are not there to be looked at, but to enable us to look through them at the view beyond, so we are not commanded to believe the Bible, but, through the window of the Bible, to see God's light." [10] No one can question the earnest piety behind Brunner's account of revelation; it remains to be seen whether it is pious nonsense.

Opposition to revelation as propositional truth was also shared by Rudolf Bultmann. Bultmann rejected the position that revelation is "the communication of knowledge or of doctrine." [11] He would have nothing to do with any view that allowed one to speak of God in "generally valid sentences . . . that are true apart from a connection to the concrete existential situation of the speaker." [12] The human agent of revelation, Bultmann maintained, never appears as a communicator of teaching. "He has imparted no information about God at all. . . . He does not *communicate anything*, but calls men to himself." [13] Neither a set of propositions nor a set of dogmas, revelation for Bultmann is an act in which God addresses his word of salvation to human beings. God's personal disclosure must produce self-understanding in the one who hears and responds to the act of revelation.

> When the revelation is truly understood as God's revelation, it is no longer a communication of teachings, nor of ethical

---

[9]See Emil Brunner, *Our Faith*, tr. John W. Rilling (New York: Scribner, 1949), p. 10.

[10]*Revelation and Reason*, pp. 181–82.

[11]H. P. Owen, *Revelation and Existence* (Cardiff: University of Wales Press, 1957), p. 66.

[12]Rudolf Bultmann, *Faith and Understanding*, tr. Louis Pettibone Smith (New York: Harper and Row, 1969), p. 26.

[13]Rudolf Bultmann, *Theology of the New Testament*, tr. Kendrick Grobel. Copyright 1951, 1955, 1979 (New York: Scribner, 1951, 1955), 2:41.

> or historical and philosophical truths, but God speaking
> directly to me, assigning me each time to the place that is
> allotted me before God, i.e., summoning me in my hu-
> manity which is null and void without God and which is
> open to God only in the recognition of its nullity. Hence
> there can be only one 'criterion' for the truth of revelation,
> namely, this, that the word which claims to be the revela-
> tion must place each man before a decision—the decision
> as to how he wants to understand himself: as one who wins
> his life and authenticity by his own resources, reason, and
> actions, or by the grace of God.[14]

Revelation then not only unveils God the speaker; it also removes the
veil from the hearers as it helps us better understand what we are and
what is our potential.[15]

Paul Tillich also adhered to the noncognitive view. For Tillich,
"there are no revealed doctrines, but there are revelatory events and
situations which can be described in doctrinal terms. . . . The 'Word of
God' contains neither revealed commandments nor revealed doctrines."[16] Avery Dulles explains that for Tillich, revelation "is a special
and extraordinary type of knowledge. It is the apprehension of the
mysterious—of that which lies beyond the grasp of man's natural powers. In revelation, indeed, God manifests himself; the human intellect is
brought face to face with the transcendent God."[17] Because God is
transcendent,

> he cannot be reached by ordinary human knowledge. In
> order to acquire any genuine knowledge of God, therefore,
> it is necessary for the mind to overleap all finite categories
> and transcend the ordinary distinctions between subject and
> object. . . . That which is revealed . . . is strict mystery. It
> cannot be apprehended by ordinary thought and, for the

---

[14]Rudolf Bultmann, *Myth and Christianity: An Inquiry into the Possibility of Religion Without Myth*, with Karl Jaspers, tr. Norbert Gutermann (New York: Noonday,
1958), p. 69.

[15]See H. P. Owen's *Revelation and Existence*, p. 88.

[16]Paul Tillich, *Systematic Theology*, 3 vols. (Chicago: University of Chicago Press,
1951), 1: 125.

[17]Avery Dulles, S. J., "Paul Tillich and the Bible," in *Paul Tillich in Catholic
Thought*, ed. Thomas A. O'Meara, O.P., and Celestin D. Weisser, O.P. (London: Dar-
ton, Longman & Todd, 1965), p. 110.

same reason, it cannot be expressed in ordinary language. Propositions about revelations are not themselves revelatory.[18]

Tillich denigrates propositions as a vehicle of revelation. "Propositions," he wrote, "have no revelatory power."[19] "If the 'Word of God' or the 'act of revelation' is called the source of systematic theology, it must be emphasized that the 'Word of God' is not limited to the words of a book and that the act of revelation is not the 'inspiring' of a 'book of revelations,' even if the book is the document of the final 'Word of God,' the fulfillment and criterion of all revelations."[20] It comes as no surprise then to find Tillich opposed to viewing the Bible as the Word of God. He wrote: "But if the Bible is called the Word of God, theological confusion is almost unavoidable. . . . Probably nothing has contributed more to the misinterpretation of all biblical doctrine of the Word than the identification of the Word with the Bible."[21]

The roll of theologians who shared the distrust of revealed knowledge goes on. H. Richard Niebuhr was typical of those American theologians who helped impart the noncognitive view of revelation to theological students on this side of the Atlantic. According to Niebuhr, the meaning of revelation "cannot be expressed in the impersonal ways of creeds or other propositions but only in responsive acts of personal character."[22] Back across the Atlantic, John Baillie left no doubt where he stood when he wrote: "God does not give us information by communication. He gives us himself in communion. It is not information about God that is revealed but . . . God himself."[23]

The noncognitive view of revelation became so dominant in nonevangelical circles that in 1966 John Hick announced confidently that "in more recent times the notion of divinely revealed propositions has virtually disappeared from Protestant theology, being replaced by the idea of revelation through history."[24] Hick summarizes the official doctrine:

[18]Ibid., pp. 110–11.

[19]Tillich, *Systematic Theology*, 1:127.

[20]Ibid., p. 35.

[21]Ibid., pp. 158–59.

[22]H. Richard Niebuhr, *The Meaning of Revelation* (New York: Macmillan, 1962), p. 112.

[23]John Baillie, *The Idea of Revelation in Recent Thought* (New York: Columbia University Press, 1956), p. 29.

[24]John Hick, *Faith and Knowledge*, 2nd ed. (Ithaca, New York: Cornell University Press, 1966), p. 30.

> Revelation is not a divine promulgation of propositions, nor is faith a believing of such propositions. The theological propositions formulated on the basis of revelation have a secondary status. They do not constitute the content of God's self-revelation but are human and therefore fallible verbalizations, constructed to aid both the integration of our religious experience into our own minds and the communication of religious experience to others.[25]

All of this would have come as surprising news to the Reformers, to Aquinas and Anselm, to Augustine, to the fathers of the church, as well as to Paul and the other human authors of the New Testament. I do not deny that the noncognitive view of revelation contains important moments of truth. I shall leave unanswered the question whether those moments of truth are cognitive or noncognitive. Certainly, the personal dimension of revelation is important. Moreover, the dynamic and present element of revelation must be emphasized. Revelation is not a static thing that belongs exclusively to the past. God's revelation must become alive and dynamic in the present experience of the believer, through the action of the Holy Spirit. The weakness of the noncognitive approach to revelation lies not so much in what its advocates affirmed as in what they ignored or denied. Ignoring *belief that*, they emphasized faith in the sense of *belief in*. But *belief in* has *belief that* as a necessary condition.

---

[25]Ibid., pp. 28–29.

Chapter 4

A Defense of Propositional Revelation

The noncognitive or nonpropositional view of revelation that has been dominant in nonevangelical Protestant theology for so long seemed more persuasive than it should have for one basic reason. Proponents of the noncognitive view misrepresented (unintentionally, I believe) the alternative to their position.

IMPORTANT LOGICAL DISTINCTIONS

Actually, four possible positions on the issue of cognitive revelation are possible. Their relationship can be illustrated with the help of a device borrowed from Aristotle. Aristotle used what he called the Square of Opposition to indicate the logical relationships that exist between the four basic kinds of categorical propositions. The four kinds of propositions and their place in the Square of Opposition are as follows:

(A) ALL S IS P   (E) NO S IS P

(I) SOME S IS P   (O) SOME S IS NOT P

For convenience, Aristotle named the four kinds of propositions the A, E, I, and O propositions. He also had names for the logical entailments that can exist among the propositions. For our purposes, the only relationship we need to consider is that of contradiction, the relationship that exists between A and O, and between the E and I propositions. When two propositions are contradictory, it follows that if one is true, the other is necessarily false; and if one is false; the other is necessarily true.

43

Applying Aristotle's Square of Opposition to the four possible positions on the issue of cognitive revelation, we get the following:

(A) ALL REVELATION IS PROPOSITIONAL.	(E) NO REVELATION IS PROPOSITIONAL.
(I) SOME REVELATION IS PROPOSITIONAL.	(O) SOME REVELATION IS NOT PROPOSITIONAL.

For the purposes of our discussion, the view stated by the O proposition is unimportant and will be ignored. The three positions we have to consider are those represented by the A, E, and I types.

As we have already seen, the view expressed by the E proposition (No revelation is propositional) expresses the dominant theory of revelation in contemporary nonevangelical Protestant theology. It is the form in which the sceptical legacy of Hume and Kant appears among their present-day theological heirs. The claim seems unassailable that modern nonevangelical theology (excepting Karl Barth) rejects any place for information or knowledge in divine revelation. We have already cited the evidence. None of the theologians quoted earlier ever made the slightest qualification to their public opposition to propositional revelation.

One of the first steps that must be taken in this matter is deciding the precise nature of the alternative to the nonpropositional thesis. Perhaps the major difference between evangelical and neo-orthodox views of revelation is the former's insistence that revelation is propositional. But this claim may take two forms, an extreme one (the A proposition) that *all* revelation is propositional and a more modest one (the I proposition) that *some* revelation is propositional. Advocates of the nonpropositional thesis (E) would have everyone think that the evangelical alternative to their view is indeed the extreme claim that all revelation is propositional. But this is not the evangelical view, I contend, although it is indeed true that confusion about this point underlies a great deal of opposition to the evangelical and propositional view of revelation. The difficulties with the A thesis (all revelation is propositional) are obvious and overwhelming. For one thing, the theory entails positions that are, within the context of evangelical theology, either absurd or heretical.

Classical Christian orthodoxy certainly wishes to maintain that God reveals truth and that knowledge of this truth is an essential component in personal relationship to the Creator. But it is equally clear that some divine revelation assumes forms that are not propositional. God is revealed, for example, in divine acts that have occurred in history such as the Exodus and the Resurrection. But it is foolish to think of such acts or events as propositions. A hypothetical advocate of the extreme A position might attempt to reply that the historical event cannot be revelation apart from interpretations of the event, interpretations that must be expressed in propositions. I concede this, but also insist on making a common sense distinction between a revelatory event which cannot be a proposition and any accompanying interpretation which is.

Moreover, Jesus Christ is the living Word of God. God is revealed in the very person of Jesus. The A position entails that if God is revealed in Jesus, then Jesus is a proposition. God also reveals Himself personally to people in encounters that cannot be converted straight into propositions. Paul reported that he had such an experience (most interpreters think Paul was writing about himself), but he found it impossible to give a report of the experience (2 Cor. 12:1–4). People can know other people personally in ways that transcend the powers of human language.

I conclude, therefore, that it is a serious error to interpret the evangelical doctrine of propositional revelation as identical with the view that all revelation is propositional. While Jesus Christ is a revelation of God, he clearly is not a proposition; nor are the events in which God revealed Himself.

The evangelical doctrine of propositional revelation should be understood then as the contradictory of the neo-orthodox thesis that no revelation is propositional. The contradictory of this E proposition is the I, namely, *some* revelation is propositional, some revelation conveys cognitive information. Basic to the evangelical position is the claim that we *can* have cognitive information about God. Since a proposition is the minimal vehicle of truth, the information about God is contained, in this view, in divinely revealed propositions. Note again that this position *does not* claim that *all* revelation must be cognitive or reducible to human language. It asserts only that some revelation is cognitive and has been expressed in human language. That some revelation is personal and noncognitive and that some revelation (such as God's revelation through His mighty acts in history) is compatible with the evangelical position.

Evangelicals must make it clear that they believe revelation can be both personal *and* cognitive. Orthodoxy contends that the ultimate object of revelation is God, not just some truth about God. Whatever God reveals and whichever means He uses in revelation, His purpose is to bring people into a personal, saving, loving, serving relationship with Himself.

The noncognitive E thesis (no revelation is propositional) is simplistic. It assumes that language and truth are somehow incompatible with personal knowledge, whereas in fact they are indispensable components of most personal knowledge.

> It is true that our personalities cannot be compressed into propositions. It is also true that unless we express ourselves in language, our attempts to express ourselves become a dumb charade. To deprive a person of language and the capacity to make himself articulate is to make that person sub-personal. There is no *a priori* reason why the personal God should not be able to express Himself in personal language. And the biblical writers attest this.[1]

Claims by writers like Temple or Brunner that revelation is exclusively personal and never propositional do not "make God more personal, but . . . make Him less so."[2]

PERSONAL AND PROPOSITIONAL

Evangelicalism insists that personal knowledge of God is not in competition with propositional knowledge about God. The more person A *knows about* person B, the better A can *know* B *in a personal way*. What kind of encounter could take place between two blind, deaf, and dumb people who had absolutely no information about each other? God does not treat humankind in this impersonal way. Scripture declares that people require information about God that He has taken the initiative to supply (Heb. 11:6; John 20:30; 1 John 1:1–3). Personal

---

[1]Taken from *Karl Barth and the Christian Message* by Colin Brown. © 1967 by Tyndale Press, London, and used by permission of InterVarsity Press, Downers Grove, IL 60515, USA., pp. 43–44.

[2]Ibid., p. 44.

encounter cannot take place in a cognitive vacuum. Saving faith presupposes some genuine knowledge about God (Rom. 10:9; 1 Cor. 15:1–4).

But, neo-orthodoxy counters, there is at least one catch to all this. The disjunction between personal and propositional revelation *is* exclusive, it insists, because cognitive knowledge about God is unattainable. Because God is totally transcendent, because He is unlike anything else in human experience, human language is an unfit instrument to capture ideas or express truths about God. Nor are human rational faculties adequate for knowledge about the transcendent. Cognitive knowledge about God is an impossible dream. This should be a familiar theme by now. It is of course nothing but a restatement of Hume's Gap and Kant's Wall. The implication is that God could not communicate genuine information about Himself even if He wanted to.

On this issue, neo-orthodoxy takes a radical all-or-nothing position. Since, on its view, revealed knowledge about the transcendent God is impossible, revelation must be personal encounter; there is no alternative. Less extreme, orthodoxy affirms that some revelation is encounter and some revelation is communication. The two modes of revelation complement each other. To experience genuine encounter requires information about God and about human need for God. In order to distinguish genuine encounter from the ever-present threat of spurious religious experience, we need information about God. We need information about how to manifest love for God. And we need divinely given interpretations of God's mighty acts in history if we are to penetrate beyond a historical enigma to the truth.

Scripture recognizes a distinction between true and false doctrine. Those who preach false doctrine are worthy of God's most severe judgment (Gal. 1:6–9; 1 John 4:1; 5:10–12). The Christian is obliged to recognize this distinction. But just how does the Christian come to know true doctrine? Those who deny propositional revelation argue that the cognitive assertions that constitute church doctrine arise from reflection about a noncognitive encounter, one that discloses no information. But if this is true, if God never reveals truth to man, where does the neo-orthodox theologian receive *his* information from? And what is the source of the truth that the New Testament deems such an important part of genuine Christian commitment? If revelation has no informational content, how can it yield doctrine?

James Orr expressed great puzzlement over alleged Christian theologians who disparage the doctrinal element of Christianity. "If there is a religion in the world which exalts the office of teaching, it is safe to say that it is the religion of Jesus Christ."[3] As unimportant as doctrine is in most pagan religions, Orr continued, "this is precisely where Christianity distinguishes itself from other religions—it does contain doctrine. It comes to men with definite, positive teaching; it claims to be the truth; it bases religion on knowledge, though a knowledge which is only attainable under moral conditions."[4] Orr was amazed that anyone approaching the New Testament with discernment could be sceptical about the importance of doctrine for Christianity. "A religion based on mere feeling is the vaguest, most unreliable, most unstable of all things. A strong, stable, religious life can be built up on no other ground than that of intelligent conviction. . . . Christianity, therefore, addresses itself to the intelligence as well as to the heart."[5]

One can hardly accuse evangelical authors of being silent about the dual nature of divine revelation, that is, that revelation has both cognitive and personal dimensions. H. D. McDonald, for one, began the second of his two studies of the subject by expressing regret about the tendency to exaggerate one dimension to the exclusion of the other.

> On the one hand, there was with some, such a strong emphasis upon the objective aspect that revelation came to be regarded as a body of Divinely communicated truths stated in strict propositional fashion to which all that was needed was to give the appropriate mental acknowledgement. . . . Such an understanding of revelation left it soulless. It was something without heart and spirit. . . . On the other hand, there were those who with resentment and ridicule regarded the idea of revelation as existing *ab extra* as the worst of all follies and the wickedest of all fancies. To such, revelation was essentially and entirely subjective. . . . Such an under-

---

[3]James Orr, *The Christian View of God and the World*, 7th ed. (New York: Scribner, 1904), p. 20.
[4]Ibid.
[5]Ibid., pp. 20–21.

standing of revelation, however, left it without any truth-content: and tended to substitute individual feelings for historical facts.[6]

McDonald's conclusions coincide with mine. He thinks "the right relation between the objective and the subjective in religion is an issue of the most fundamental importance and an inquiry demanding the greatest urgency. Whenever the balance between these two becomes upset, then some element of the full truth is inevitably lost."[7] McDonald rejects any attempt to set up a divorce between the Holy Spirit and the Scriptures.

> No ultimate antithesis between "Spirit" and "Truth" is possible. . . . It is not a case of the Spirit without the Scriptures, nor is it a case of the Scriptures without the Spirit. The Spirit cannot do His work without the Scriptures and the Scriptures cannot do theirs without the Spirit. Revelation is not a matter of Spirit only, but of Spirit and Truth. God's word is "truth," God's work is by the "Spirit." The two go together.[8]

This implies, for McDonald, that "a Scripture without the Spirit makes for a fruitless faith, while the Spirit without the Scriptures makes for an undisciplined faith. The one makes for a dead orthodoxy, while the other leads to an unrestrained enthusiasm. The first gives lifelessness to the Church; and the second, license to the individual."[9] Revelation can never be either spirit or truth; it must be both.

SOME COMMON MISUNDERSTANDINGS ABOUT PROPOSITIONAL REVELATION

The interpretation of the doctrine of propositional revelation that we have advanced defuses the objections most commonly raised to the doctrine and unmasks them as confusions or misrepresentations of the position. What are these objections and confusions?

First of all, propositional revelation should not be confused with

---

[6]H. D. McDonald, *Theories of Revelation, An Historical Study: 1860–1960* (Grand Rapids: Baker, 1963), p. 7.

[7]Ibid., p. 342.

[8]Ibid., p. 343.

[9]Ibid., p. 344.

the quite separate doctrine of verbal inspiration. Theoretically, a person could accept propositional revelation but reject verbal inspiration. The converse would not be true. The doctrine of verbal inspiration has to do with the extent to which God's revelation is conveyed in *words*, notably the written words of the Bible. It has to do with the role of the Holy Spirit in guiding the human authors of Scripture in their selection of words to convey the inspired ideas.* The doctrine of propositional revelation expresses a conviction on a quite different question: Is God's revelation a disclosure of truth? Does it have cognitive content?

The advocate of propositional revelation does not hold that God's written revelation must assume a particular literary form. Countless critics have assumed that if one accepts propositional revelation, one must also believe that all written revelation assumes the form of *assertions*. Comparatively little of the Bible is written in this form. Scripture contains more than historical assertions or doctrinal statements. God uses human language as a medium of revelation, and language has many different functions. Language can be used assertively to teach (consider the Book of Romans) or to record history (consider the Book of Acts). Language may be used to command (Matt. 28:19–20), to exhort (Rom. 12:1–2), or to proclaim (Matt. 5:1–10). God uses poetry and allegory as well.

While all Scripture is inspired, not all Scripture is concerned to declare truth in sentences that are to be interpreted literally. The Evangelical believes that all Scripture is inspired by God and is profitable for teaching, for reproof, for correction, and for training in righteousness (2 Tim. 3:16). But there is no need to assume that this list is exhaustive. It may be only illustrative of the multiple functions of language in Scripture.

The orthodox view does not lead to "bibliolatry"—the veneration of the Bible with a reverence appropriate only to God. It is difficult to see how even the most crude, unimaginative theory of mechanical dictation would justify the charge of bibliolatry. Perhaps the critic means to suggest that because Evangelicals regard the Bible as the Word of God, they are in danger of diverting from God the reverence and honor due Him. But is any person of normal intelligence likely to do

---

*None of this, of course, entails the mechanical view of dictation frequently and erroneously attributed to all Evangelicals.

this? If a king issued a proclamation, those of his subjects who honored and reverenced him would hardly show their respect for the king's person by ignoring his words or by denying that he had even spoken. What sensible person would confuse honor for the king's person with honor for his word? It is precisely the fact that genuine knowledge is available about the nature and the will of God that makes bibliolatry sin. True revelation of God's nature, character, and will enables us to know the difference between worshiping Almighty God and worshiping a book.

Nor does belief in propositional revelation mean that one denies the human element in Scripture. God used human authors whose writings reflect their personal backgrounds, personalities, distinctive vocabulary, and cultural milieu. Acceptance of propositional revelation does not subvert the notion of faith as personal commitment to God by confusing it with the notion of faith as an acceptance of true propositions. "Because man is 'spiritual,' revelation must come as 'Spirit,' and because he is 'rational,' revelation must come as 'Truth.' This means that, as a final fact, revelation will be, not one to the exclusion of the other, but at the same time both."[10]

It is also wrong to suppose that the doctrine of propositional revelation minimizes revelation in the sense of *event*. God does reveal Himself in His mighty acts in history. But even though God's acts in history may be a type of nonpropositional revelation, these acts require a divinely given interpretation.

> According to the Bible, the meaning of the mighty acts of God, including that crowning act of all—God incarnate in Jesus Christ, is not a humanly drawn conclusion based on observation of these acts; rather, the meaning of the act is itself also a divine revelation—God's interpretation of His own divine acts. This revelatory word is given by God to man in just as objective a form as are the acts of God in history. These revelations of truth represent God's interpretations. They are God's meaning of events in history. . . . Biblical revelation is a continuous interdependent unity of act-revelation and truth-revelation.[11]

[10]McDonald, *Theories of Revelation*, p. 284.
[11]Kenneth Kantzer in *Jesus of Nazareth: Savior and Lord*, ed. Carl F. H. Henry (Grand Rapids: Eerdmans, 1966), p. 257.

The Evangelical agrees with Oscar Cullmann when he says that "revelation consists in both—in the event as such and in its interpretation. . . . Not only the interpretation but also the event is regarded as revelation."[12] The Romans crucified thousands of Jews. From the perspective of event, the crucifixion of Jesus was simply one more instance of Roman legal practice, and many eyewitnesses of the death of Jesus interpreted His crucifixion from this perspective. Similarly, many theologians accept the historicity of Jesus' crucifixion but fail to see it as God's atonement for sin. Only through the perspective of God's revelation is Jesus' death seen as what it is—the decisive point in the history of redemption. Biblical revelation is a conjunction of event and the interpretation of that event.

Belief in a propositional revelation need not involve a reduction of God's revelation to something static. Plato realized there was a problem whenever ideas were put into writing: matters reduced to writing die in some sense while the spoken word lives on. This observation should not be taken lightly. God's revelation is not static or dead; it is a gracious *act* of God. Evangelicals must beware lest their emphasis on revelation inscripturated in human language should degenerate into a de-emphasis of the living and active nature of God's speaking. The God whose voice can raise the dead is not one who can be limited by "dead" words. The activity of the Spirit of God insures the vitality of God's revelation. God speaks and His word is recorded. He continues to speak through that record; and those words live, energized by the Spirit of God.

The role of the Spirit raises the issue of the relation between the objective and subjective poles of revelation. It is one thing for revelation to be objectively given through divinely aided speakers. It is quite another for that revelation to be received and understood. Neoorthodoxy over-emphasized the subjective side of revelation at the expense of its objective side. Evangelicals must reject the claim that Scripture is not revelation but only becomes revelation when illuminated by the Spirit. They must remember that *revelation* can refer both to the act of revealing (the subjective side) and to that which is revealed (the objective side). Evangelicals insist that both God's act of revealing and the inspired record of that revelation are necessary.

---

[12]Oscar Cullmann, "The Resurrection: Event and Meaning," *Christianity Today,* 9 (March 26, 1965): 8.

> The revelation is, of course, prior to the record. First the life then the literature which embodies and secures the original revelation for subsequent generations. If there were no adequate record then would each new age need again the revelation. . . . The record is necessary if the revelation is to be preserved. The revelation of God in Christ would not have been guaranteed to those who followed unless He completed it in an adequate medium of transmission.[13]

Perhaps the following example will help clarify the relation between the objective and subjective dimensions of revelation. Imagine that a mother and her child are separated in a time of war. By chance, years later, the mother and her son, now an adult, live, unrecognized by each other, in the same village. The one person who knew their real relationship (knew the truth about their relationship) kept it to himself until he decided to reveal the truth in a letter. But that person died before the letter was delivered, and the letter remained hidden for years. Suppose finally that the letter was discovered and the actual relationship of the mother and son was revealed. Certainly there is an important sense in which the revelation was contained objectively in the letter. But it is also true that the relationship between the mother and son was revealed *to them* only after certain conditions were realized. The neo-orthodox theologian may insist that the only revelation that counts is the subjective one. No one should deny, perhaps, that it is the important revelation. But the subjective revelation could not have taken place unless the truth about the relationship between mother and son had been objectively revealed in the letter. When speaking about Scripture, it is important to affirm the objective character of God's revelation. The basic error of religious subjectivists is that they confuse the proclamation or delivery of truth with the reception of truth.

It is sobering to remember that the phrase *propositional revelation* has been in use for only forty years or so, and that it probably was not coined by Evangelicals. One of the earliest references to the distinction between personal and propositional revelation occurs in a review of Emil Brunner's book, *The Divine-Human Encounter*.[14] The phrase *propositional revelation* seems to have been used by non-Evangelicals as

---

[13]McDonald, *Ideas of Revelation*, p. 192.
[14]The review by E. G. Homrighausen appeared in *Theology Today* in 1944.

a term of derision for the position they wished to repudiate. Evangelicals gradually picked up the phrase in the late 1940's and it stuck.

Given the parentage of the phrase, then, there should be no sentimental attachment to it on the part of Evangelicals. Perhaps another word or phrase will gain acceptance, one that more successfully avoids suggesting that an exclusive disjunction exists between encounter and knowledge. Until then, however, it will probably continue to be necessary to use *propositional revelation*. But all who discuss the position should not equate revealed propositions with sentences; and they should remember that what the position entails is the belief that some revelatory acts have a cognitive or informational character, and that this revealed truth is deposited in the various literary forms found in the Bible.

Chapter 5

A Brief But Necessary Interlude

A brief review of the territory already covered will be helpful as we look forward to the terrain yet to be explored. I have been investigating the history and development of the claim that whatever else revelation or the Word of God may be, it cannot be the communication of information.

Specifically, we saw how David Hume and Immanuel Kant came to hold that human knowledge about God is impossible. We then traced their influence to Schleiermacher and Ritschl and through them to Protestant liberalism. The neo-orthodox theologians who came on the scene after World War I saw their own work as an antidote to the immanentism and subjectivism of liberalism and an alternative to the uninformed biblicism (as they saw it) of conservative Protestants. But neo-orthodoxy was actually an extension of the theological agnosticism I call Hume's Gap and Kant's Wall. With the exception of the later Barth, the full complement of thinkers we noted, ranging from the neo-orthodox Brunner to the existentialist Bultmann, rejected any possibility of human knowledge about God. They consciously repudiated any place for truth or knowledge in their view of revelation. But their noncognitive view of revelation conflicts with the church's historic understanding of revelation, raises insoluble problems, and gains plausibility for itself by misrepresenting its major competition, the evangelical theory of propositional revelation. The fundamental ground that supports this noncognitive view of revelation is the conviction that the mind of man is incapable of knowing the mind of God.

I disagree with this position. And for support I shall appeal (in chapter 6) to a doctrine that played a prominent role in early Christian thought—the Logos doctrine. Use of this classical theory gives additional depth to the discussion, for with it the question becomes: What is the relationship between the logos of God and the mind of man?

So far, my argument has of necessity been negative and critical. My task can now become positive and constructive as I explicate a conviction of the early church from which modern theology has unfortunately strayed: That the human mind can know the divine mind. The early church expressed this conviction in its expansion of the New Testament teaching that Christ is the Logos who makes all human knowledge possible. A proper recovery from the faulty epistemology of much contemporary theology requires a return to the Logos doctrine (the subject of chapter 6).

A great deal of confusion exists about Christian rationalism, the theory of knowledge that grounds many of the claims that will be made in this book. Therefore, before explaining the continuation of the Logos doctrine in the Christian rationalism of St. Augustine (chapter 8), and in order to eliminate some of this confusion, I will briefly examine the classic debate between rationalism and empiricism (chapter 7). Among other things, I will be asking such questions as: What is an innate idea? Are there any innate ideas? And, if there are, how are they related to God and to the human logos? One of the central concerns of chapter 7 is the explanation and defense of the notion of an innate idea. The differences between these two theories of knowledge will be discussed and I will offer reasons for the one that I believe is correct. I do not presume to solve all of the complex and vexing problems generated by these topics. But we must look briefly at these two basic options in epistemology, for the topic is knowledge of God.

Chapter 8 will investigate the more important elements of Augustine's (A.D. 354–430) Christian rationalism and note the points at which he was influenced by Plato and Plotinus. What is crucial in Augustine's position for this study is his conviction that all of his theorizing about the foundations of human knowledge was an attempt to draw out the more general epistemological implications of the Logos doctrine. In Augustine's writings a Christian theory of knowledge may be seen emerging from the Logos doctrine.

Chapter 9 addresses the peculiar distrust of reason and logic that one finds in the writings of so many modern religious thinkers. This religious revolt against logic does Christian theism a great disservice. Consequently, chapter 10 argues that Christian theists should be the last people to discard the principle of noncontradiction. I am especially critical of the widely held view that God's logic is different from human logic. Chapter 11 ties together the basic elements of a Christian theory of knowledge by showing how human language can be a fit instrument to express divinely revealed truth. In the last chapter, I provide several examples of contemporary Evangelicals who reject the position of this book and thus, in my opinion, lapse into a variety of errors.

Chapter 6

The Christian Logos

As we have seen, the allegation that a radical disparity exists between the transcendent divine mind and the finite mind of human beings is a fundamental postulate of the theological agnosticism that pervades much contemporary theology. An adequate alternative to this sceptical position requires the development of an ontology and epistemology that will bridge the alleged gap. Fortunately, no new theory is required. The answers to this problem can be found in the Logos doctrine of the early church. Jesus Christ, the eternal Logos of God, mediates all divine revelation and grounds the correspondence between the divine and human minds. This eternal Logos is a necessary condition for the communication of revealed truth; indeed, it is a necessary condition for human knowledge about anything. From the beginning of Christianity, it was believed that reason and logic have cosmic significance.

This chapter will investigate the Logos doctrine as expressed by Alexandrian Judaism, the New Testament, and the early fathers of the church. It aims to discover what light this doctrine can throw on the question: How can the mind of man know the mind of God? Since the Greeks used *logos* as a synonym for mind or reason, the question can now be worded: How can the human logos know the divine Logos?

One of the most puzzling aspects of the New Testament teaching about the Logos is its relationship to the use of the term in earlier thinkers, especially the first-century Jewish philosopher Philo.* Philo

---

*No specific dates for Philo's birth and death are available. It is thought that he died about A.D. 50.

was not the first to write about a cosmic Logos. For Heraclitus of Ephesus (who flourished about 500 B.C.) as well as the Stoic philosophers who came along much later, Logos was a cosmic law of Reason that controls the universe and is immanent in human reason. The Stoics regarded human reason as an extension of the Reason that pervades the entire cosmos. It is important to note that the Logos of Heraclitus and the Stoics was neither a personal God nor even a personal being but a metaphysical abstraction. Philo was influenced both by this earlier speculation about the Logos and by Plato's teaching about the Forms, which Philo interpreted as thoughts of God.

Alexandria, Egypt, was a dominant locale of the Jewish Diaspora and the chief center of Hellenistic thought at the beginning of the Christian era. It is not surprising that the Jews who lived there were open to influence from concepts in Greek philosophy that seemed consistent with their religious beliefs. The compatibility of Judaism with both Platonism and Stoicism seemed especially obvious to the man who became the most well-known intellectual of the Alexandrian community, Philo Judaeus.

Some of Philo's reinterpretations of Plato made it easier for later Christian thinkers to use Platonism as a philosophical framework for their Christian world-views. Plato himself did not make clear the precise relationship between the eternal Forms and his God. But once Philo began to explain the Forms as thoughts of God, it became possible to think of the Forms as both eternal and created. The Forms are created in the sense that God is a necessary condition for their existence; if God did not exist, the Forms would not exist. Since the Forms subsist in the mind of God, they are ontologically dependent upon God for their existence. But since God is eternal and the Forms are His eternal ideas, the Forms are also eternal. They are eternal thoughts of God which serve as an archetypal pattern for the corporeal world. Philo gave the name *Logos* both to the mind of God and to the thoughts of God (the Forms). As Gordon H. Clark suggests, the "Logos passes from a stage internal in the mind of God to a stage external as a really existing world of Ideas, and even to a third stage in which it becomes immanent in the sensible world."[1] As Clark explains further,

---

[1]Gordon H. Clark, *Thales to Dewey* (Grand Rapids: Baker, 1981), p. 202.

the first and most universal of all the powers or ideas is the Logos. As the thought of God the Logos . . . comprehends the whole intelligible world. Sometimes Philo's wording seems to imply that the Logos is a thinking soul rather than the world of Ideas. Apart from the literary device of personification, this mode of expression can be explained in virtue of a contrast between God and men. An architect, for example, has many plans, his human logos thinks many thoughts, and accordingly it is easy to distinguish between his reason and one of his thoughts. But God has one plan only, and reason or the Logos can be both a power and the world of Ideas.[2]

Either Philo or one of his contemporaries in Alexandria sought to bring Judaism and Hellenistic philosophy closer by merging the Greek notion of Logos with the Jewish idea of Wisdom (*Sophia*). In Philo's writings, *Logos*, *Sophia*, and *Nous* are all used interchangeably.[3] Henry Austryn Wolfson acknowledges the interchangeability of *Logos* and *Sophia* in Philo's writings.

Wisdom, then, is only another word for Logos, and it is used in all the senses of the term Logos. Both these mean, in the first place, a property of God, identical with His essence, and like His essence, eternal. In the second place, they mean a real, incorporeal being, created by God before the creation of the world. Third . . . Logos means also a Logos immanent in the world. . . . Finally, Logos is also used by Philo in the sense of one of its constituent ideas, such, for instance, as the idea of mind.[4]

The use of the word *logos* in the Gospel of John understandably gave rise to questions about a possible relation between the writer of the fourth Gospel and Alexandrian Judaism. Several decades ago, it was

---

[2]Gordon H. Clark, *Selections from Hellenistic Philosophy* (New York: Appleton-Century-Crofts, 1940), pp. 156–57.

[3]Philo, *Allegorical Interpretation* I, 19, 65.

[4]Henry Austryn Wolfson, *Philo* (Cambridge, Mass.: Harvard University Press, 1962), 1:258. See also Wolfson's *Religious Philosophy: A Group of Essays* (New York: Atheneum, 1965), pp. 35–36. It should be made clear that the various Philonic authorities frequently disagree over quite central issues. Also to be consulted are the works of Edwin R. Goodenough, especially his *By Light, Light* (Amsterdam: Philo Press, 1969) and his *An Introduction to Philo Judaeus* (Oxford: Basil Blackwell, 1962).

fashionable in some circles to suggest that the writer of John's Gospel was directly influenced by the Alexandrian Logos doctrine. What was apparently unrecognized by some of these theorists was the fact that a similar Logos doctrine is also present in the Epistle to the Hebrews. In fact, a careful study of Hebrews reveals a number of remarkable similarities between the concepts of Mediator and Logos in the Book of Hebrews and notions prominent in the philosophical and theological world of discourse in Alexandrian Judaism. It seems obvious that the writer and readership of Hebrews shared a common background with Alexandrian Jews like Philo.

The writer of Hebrews demonstrates a familiarity with the tenets of Hellenistic Judaism as these are known from documents which were written in Alexandria. Consequently, he (or she) knew the Platonic philosophy that Hellenistic Jews like Philo had sought to harmonize with Judaism.[5] The writer of Hebrews certainly knew the Alexandrian teachings about Divine Wisdom (Sophia) and the Logos. In particular, the writer of Hebrews evidences familiarity with the Alexandrian work, *The Wisdom of Solomon*. Although the extent of the writer's knowledge of Philo's thought and writings is debateable, at the very least the writer of Hebrews shared with Philo a common education in Alexandrian thought. Moreover, the writer assumes that the reader is familiar with Alexandrian theology and philosophy. The view that the Epistle to the Hebrews is a legacy to Christianity from the Hellenized Judaism of Alexandria is shared by a number of New Testament scholars.[6]

Two drastically opposed views concerning the relationship between the Epistle to the Hebrews and the thought of Philo and Alexandrian Judaism presently compete for attention. The one extreme, typified by

---

[5]George Barker Stevens does not hesitate to affirm that the writer of Hebrews "was a literary Hellenist, who was familiar with the philosophical ideas which were current at Alexandria and practiced in the argumentative use of the Septuagint. . . . The author of the Epistle to the Hebrews was strongly imbued with Platonic and Alexandrian thought." *The Theology of the New Testament* (Edinburgh: T. & T. Clark, 1968 reprint), pp. 484, 488.

[6]Ronald Williamson cites most of the important sources on both sides of the question in the first chapter of his *Philo and the Epistle to the Hebrews* (Leiden: E. J. Brill, 1970). Contemporary Evangelicals like F. F. Bruce have not been reluctant to point out the apparent familiarity of the writer of Hebrews with some teachings of Plato. See F. F. Bruce, *The Epistle to the Hebrews* (Grand Rapids: William B. Eerdmans, 1964), pp. lxix *et passim*, as well as Bruce's commentary on Hebrews in *Peake's Commentary on the Bible*, ed. by M. Black and H. H. Rowley, rev. ed. (New York: Nelson, 1962), p. 1008.

C. Spicq,[7] holds that the author of Hebrews was definitely influenced in a direct manner by the writings of Philo. The writer may have known Philo personally, had certainly read some of Philo's writings, and may have been a Philonic convert to Christianity. More moderate versions of this thesis have found expression in the literature about Hebrews for years. Spicq's commentary on Hebrews remains one of the most detailed and fully documented works arguing for a strong, direct Philonic influence on Hebrews.

Recently however, Ronald Williamson has challenged Spicq's contentions. Williamson succeeds in pointing out a large number of weaknesses in the case built by Spicq. In his effort to rule out any Philonic influence, Williamson strays too far in the opposite direction. But he is correct in his claim that interpreters have tended to exaggerate Philo's influence on the Book of Hebrews. Williamson concludes: "The writer of Hebrews had never been a Philonist, had never read Philo's works, had never come under the influence of Philo directly or indirectly."[8]

Fortunately, we do not have to choose simply between the extremes of Spicq and Williamson. In spite of Williamson's strong antipathy to a Philonic influence on Hebrews, he is forced to admit that the writer of Hebrews "almost certainly lived and moved in circles where, in broad, general terms, ideas such as those we meet in Philo's works were known and discussed: he drew upon the same fund of cultured Greek vocabulary upon which Philo drew."[9] Williamson's important study cannot be ignored. It is no longer possible glibly to presuppose a Philonic background to every concept and term in Hebrews that has affinities to Philo. But whatever the actual relationship between the writer of Hebrews and Philo, they both share the common heritage of the Hellenistic Judaism of Alexandria.

The Epistle to the Hebrews does not apply the name Logos to Jesus any more than it explicitly calls Jesus Sophia. But there can be no mistake about Hebrews containing an implicit Logos Christology. Predicates which, in the pertinent Alexandrian literature, are applied to both Logos and Sophia, are applied by the writer of Hebrews to Jesus

---

[7]C. Spicq, *L'Épître aux Hebreux* (Paris, 1952).
[8]Ronald Williamson, p. 579.
[9]Ibid., p. 493.

(for example, Heb. 1:3: "The radiance of his glory, the exact representation of his nature"). It is clear that the writer believes that Jesus is the true Logos and Sophia.

Philo wrote of the Logos as "Mediator" (*mesitēs*)[10] and "Image" (*eikon*)[11] of God.[12] The world was created through the agency of the Logos.[13] Philo described the Logos as neither unbegotten (like God) nor begotten (like a human).[14] As such the Logos is on the borderline between God and humankind, mediating from God to humans like an ambassador and from humanity to God as a suppliant.[15] The Logos is called the First-born Son (cf. Heb. 1:6) and the Chief born.[16] The Logos is both Light[17] and the very shadow of God.[18]

The appearance of some of these as predicates of Christ (for example, mediator, first-born, radiance) in Hebrews makes it highly likely that the writer of Hebrews was familiar with the Alexandrian Logos doctrine. Even Williamson admits that Hebrews contains "a rudimentary form of Logos Christology."[19]

Similarities between the thought-world of ancient Alexandria and two of the most important books of the New Testament (Hebrews and the Gospel of John) were bound to suggest to some that a relation of dependence existed. Some went so far as to suggest that the New Testament writings in question were clearly dependent on Philo and were an accommodation of an early Christian teaching about Jesus to a highly theoretical construction of Alexandrian Judaism. Too many differences exist, however, to permit this simplistic view.

For one thing, the Logos of Hebrews and of the Gospel of John is not the metaphysical abstraction of Philo but a specific individual, a

---

[10]See Philo's *Who Is the Heir of Divine Things* 205–6. A. Oepke discusses the nuances of Philo's use of *mesitēs*. Gerhard Kittel and Gerhard Friedrich, eds. *Theological Dictionary of the New Testament*, 9 vols. (Grand Rapids: Eerdmans, 1964–73) 4:602.

[11]Cf. Hebrews 1:3 where the parallel term *charakter* occurs.

[12]See Philo's *On the Special Laws* 1, 81; *On the Sacrifices of Abel and Cain* 8; *On the Migration of Abraham* 6; *On the Unchangeableness of God* 57.

[13]Philo, *On Flight and Finding* 101; *On Dreams* 2, 45; *On the Special Laws* 1, 81.

[14]*Who is the Heir of Divine Things* 205–6.

[15]*On the Special Laws* 3, 62.

[16]*On the Confusion of Tongues* 146; *On Dreams* 1, 215; *On the Unchangeableness of God* 31; *On Husbandry* 51; *On Flight and Finding* 101.

[17]*On Dreams* 1, 75.

[18]*On the Special Laws* 3, 31.

[19]Williamson, p. 410.

historical person. The Logos of Philo was *not* a person. To be sure, Philo wrote about the Logos in personal terms but this was merely the personification of a metaphysical abstraction. According to A. H. Armstrong, the precise degree of the independent existence of Philo's Logos "must remain doubtful because Philo is so vague about it, and it certainly cannot be said to be a person, still less a Divine Person."[20] Armstrong goes on to add that Philo's Logos "differs entirely from the Logos of St. John's Prologue, an actual historical Person who is also Divine."[21] There is absolutely no support for the position that Philo believed the Logos to be personal, let alone a person living in history. Philo's Logos is especially lacking in the personal or messianic or soteriological traits so prominent in the Christian account of Jesus. Philo's Logos is not a person or messiah or savior but a cosmic principle postulated to solve assorted metaphysical and epistemological problems. In the words of Frederick Copleston, "in the Philonic doctrine of the Logos there is no reference to an historic man."[22]

A careful study of the Epistle to the Hebrews will make clear that while the writer was obviously familiar with the Platonism of Alexandria, he intentionally set out to contrast his understanding of the Christian message with the philosophy he himself may once have accepted and which his audience may still have found attractive. While the writer of Hebrews clearly had an original relationship to Alexandrian Platonism, his argument throughout the book reveals his determination to attack major aspects of that position in an effort to show the superiority of Christ and the Christian scheme of mediation and redemption. The philosophical theology of Alexandrian Judaism gave important place to mediators that fulfilled requirements of both Old Testament Wisdom theology and of the prevailing Platonic philosophy. One example of such a similarity between Wisdom theology and Platonic philosophy was the need within both systems for a being or beings who would mediate between God and the world. The writer of Hebrews

---

[20]A. H. Armstrong, *An Introduction to Ancient Philosophy* (Boston: Beacon Press, 1963), p. 162.

[21]Ibid.

[22]Frederick Copleston, *A History of Philosophy*, 9 vols. (Westminster, Maryland: The Newman Press, 1960), I: 459. For more on this topic, see Ronald Nash, "The Notion of Mediator in Alexandrian Judaism and the Epistle to the Hebrews," *The Westminster Theological Journal* 40 (1977): 106ff.

emphasizes the differences that make Christ superior to anything the Alexandrians had to offer.

My hypothesis about Hebrews, contrary to the viewpoints of Spicq and Williamson, is that one purpose, if not the major purpose, of the writer of Hebrews was to expose the inadequacy of the Alexandrian mediators.[23] "Jesus is superior," the writer of Hebrews affirms. "In fact, he is superior to your Alexandrian Logos and Sophia; he is superior to your angelic and priestly mediators; he is superior to Moses and Melchizedek. Jesus is the true Logos, the true Sophia, and the Great High Priest." This superiority of Jesus is demonstrated by showing significant ways in which Jesus differs from the Alexandrian *logoi*. In part, this demonstration of the superiority of Jesus may have been made necessary by the life situation of his readers. Hebrews suggests that because of pressure on the Christian community, they may have been tempted to return to one or more of the "older" mediators.

The New Testament ascribes three distinct but related functions to the Christian Logos which make it possible to speak of Christ as the cosmological Logos, the epistemological Logos, and the soteriological Logos. This is simply another way of saying that Jesus is a necessary condition for the existence of the world, for human knowledge, and for human redemption. Without Jesus, the world would never have come into existence and would not exist now; without Jesus, the human animal would never have become a creature capable of knowledge; and without Jesus, human beings would never have been redeemed from sin.

Christ is described as the cosmological and epistemological Logos in the prologue to John's Gospel. John describes Christ as the agent through whom God brought the world into existence: "In the beginning was the Logos, and the Logos was with God, and the Logos was God. He was in the beginning with God; all things were made through him, and without him was not anything made that was made" (John 1:1–3). St. Paul also describes the preexistent Christ as the mediator of creation (1 Cor. 8:6; Col. 1:16). The cosmological Logos continues to act as the intermediary in God's sustaining relationship to the world.

---

[23]This interpretation makes Hebrews similar in its intent to *The Wisdom of Solomon*, which the author of Hebrews knew. See Alexander A. DiLella, O.F.M., "Conservative and Progressive Theology: Sirach and Wisdom" in *Studies in Ancient Israelite Wisdom*, ed. James L. Crenshaw (New York: KTAV Publishing House, 1976), pp. 401–16.

After John describes Jesus as the cosmological Logos, he presents Him as the epistemological Logos. John declares that Christ was "the true light that enlightens every man" (John 1:9). In other words, the epistemological Logos is not only the mediator of divine special revelation (John 1:14), He is also the ground of *all* human knowledge.

The Epistle to the Hebrews, also, begins by noting the cosmological and epistemological functions of Christ, though the order of presentation is reversed. Hebrews begins by describing Christ as the epistemological Logos who mediated God's revelation to humankind. In past times, God spoke in various ways through the prophets. But that partial and incomplete word is now presented in its final, complete form "by a Son." This Son reveals God by being the very effulgence or radiance of His being (Heb. 1:1–3). The writer then describes Jesus as the cosmological Logos who mediates creation both as creator (Heb. 1:2) and sustainer (1:3).

To the cosmological and epistemological functions of the Logos, the Epistle to the Hebrews adds the third function, that of the soteriological Logos.[24] Humans can be redeemed and their sins forgiven only through the efforts of One who mediates between them and God. And so, after the writer of Hebrews described Jesus as cosmological and epistemological mediator, he continues: "When he had made purification for sins, he sat down at the right hand of the Majesty on high" (Heb. 1:3). As the argument of Hebrews later makes clear, this is not simply an addendum. It anticipates the primary emphasis of the book of Hebrews—soteriology (salvation). For while the cosmological and epistemological functions of the Mediator are not mentioned again in Hebrews, Christ's work as savior and redeemer is studied and examined from every possible angle. Jesus is the soteriological Logos who as both priest and sacrifice effects salvation.

The Logos doctrine occupied a prominent place in the thought of several early Fathers of the church. On the basis of John 1:9, Justin Martyr argued that every apprehension of truth (whether by believer or unbeliever) is made possible because men are related to the Logos, the

---

[24]All three of these functions can be found, in varying degrees, in Philo's thoughts. See the comments in footnotes on pp. 96–98 of Ronald H. Nash, "The Notion of Mediator in Alexandrian Judaism and the Epistle to the Hebrews," *The Westminster Theological Journal* 40 (1977): 89–115.

ground of truth.[25] As H. Chadwick explains Justin Martyr's view, "The Word and Wisdom of God, who is Christ, is also the Reason inherent in all things and especially in the rational creation. All who have thought and acted rationally and rightly have participated in Christ the Universal Logos."[26]

A further advance in the Christian Logos doctrine appears in the writings of Clement of Alexandria. Clement taught "that God bestowed upon man a rational principle which was an imitation of his own image, the Logos."[27] The presence of the image of God in man was Clement's way of explaining the "close kinship between the human mind and the universal Logos, the Son of God." It is but a short step from the African Father, Clement, to his even more famous African successor, St. Augustine, whose account of human knowledge extends the Logos teaching of Justin and Clement.

Few contemporary theologians have seen the implications of the New Testament Logos doctrine as clearly as Carl F. H. Henry. The Christian Logos doctrine, Henry believes, presupposes "an intelligible order or logos in things, an objective law which claims and binds man, and makes possible human understanding and valid knowledge. . . . The concept of the logos comprehends at once the interrelationship of thought, word, matter, nature, being and law."[28] As the Logos of God, Jesus guarantees human rationality and certifies the ability of humans to understand the Word of God. The correspondence between the mind of God and the human mind (that is grounded in the Logos) makes possible a human understanding of the divine communication of truth. "Christianity affirms that this world is a rational universe, that it is God's world; knowability of the universe is grounded in God's creation of man as a rational creature whose forms of thought correspond to the laws of logic subsisting in the mind of God, as well as to the rational character of the world as God's creation."[29] Later Henry adds, "Since

---

[25]Justin Martyr, I *Apol.* 5. 46. See the discussion in L. W. Barnard, *Justin Martyr* (Cambridge: Cambridge University Press, 1967), pp. 86ff.

[26]H. Chadwick, "Philo," in *Cambridge History of Later Greek and Early Medieval Philosophy*, ed. A. H. Armstrong (Cambridge: Cambridge University Press, 1967), p. 162.

[27]Salvatore R. C. Lilla, *Clement of Alexandria* (New York: Oxford University Press, 1971), p. 15.

[28]Carl F. H. Henry, *God, Revelation and Authority*, 3 vols. (Waco: Word Books, 1979), 3: 193.

[29]Ibid., 3: 192.

the eternal Logos himself structures the created universe and the conditions of communication, logical connections are eternally grounded in God's mind and will, and are binding for man in view of the *imago Dei*."[30]

Reason has an intrinsic relationship to God, it has cosmic significance. Christians believe the rational world is the projection of a rational God who objectifies His eternal thoughts in the creation and who endows the human creature, the apex of His creation, with the image of God which includes a structure of reason similar to God's own reason.

Rationalism and Empiricism

Many of the specific problems about human knowledge of God are extensions of more basic difficulties about human knowledge in general. It should be obvious that the answer to how human beings can attain knowledge about God cannot be separated from a more fundamental account of how they come to a knowledge about anything. Since our exploration of knowledge of God will require a consideration of more general epistemological issues sooner or later, we might just as well bite the bullet now and get this discussion out of the way.

Consider two basic epistemological positions somewhat loosely called empiricism and rationalism. For starters, the two theories can be contrasted by utilizing once again Aristotle's Square of Opposition. As we saw earlier, Aristotle believed there are four basic kinds of categorical propositions:

(A) ALL S IS P   (E) NO S IS P

(I) SOME S IS P   (O) SOME S IS NOT P

Corresponding to these four kinds of propositions are four possible theories about human knowledge:

(A) ALL HUMAN KNOWLEDGE ARISES FROM SENSE EXPERIENCE.[1]   (E) NO HUMAN KNOWLEDGE ARISES FROM SENSE EXPERIENCE.

(I) SOME HUMAN KNOWLEDGE ARISES FROM SENSE EXPERIENCE.   (O) SOME HUMAN KNOWLEDGE DOES NOT ARISE FROM SENSE EXPERIENCE.

---

[1]While the simplicity of my formulation presents several advantages, it can be faulted for being too simple. For one thing, it eliminates a major qualification of contemporary

Which of these four options should be viewed as statements of the positions we have called empiricism and rationalism? Empiricism, as we shall use the term, is identical with the A position, all human knowledge arises from sense experience. Since I use the word *rationalism* as the antonym of *empiricism*, the essence of rationalism is expressed in the O proposition that some human knowledge does *not* arise from sense experience.

The fact that a few thinkers in the history of philosophy regarded the E position (No human knowledge arises from sense experience) as their formulation of rationalism is a matter of some historical interest; but it should not draw attention away from my claim that rationalism is best understood as the more modest assertion that some human knowledge arises from a source other than sense experience. The more extreme E position was usually held by thinkers who held the standards of knowledge so high that no human awareness to which sensation made any contribution could qualify as knowledge. In other words, they simply defined knowledge so as to eliminate sensation as a source of knowledge. Some philosophers, like Plato for example, apparently held the E position that no knowledge arises from sense experience; but they could do this only because they defined knowledge so narrowly that only states of consciousness that excluded all sense experience could possibly satisfy their criteria of knowledge. It is worth noting that the Christian Platonist, St. Augustine, believed that knowledge (scientia) could sometimes arise through the senses.[2]

As I see it, being a rationalist does not require one to believe that every single item of human knowledge comes from a source other than

---

empiricism, namely, the admission that human knowledge of logical and mathematical truths is not derived from sense experience. Contemporary empiricists like the Logical Positivists went on to maintain that the truths of mathematics and logic are tautologies. That is, they are redundant statements that convey no new information about reality. This factor could be plugged into our formulation by making the A proposition read "All nontautological human knowledge arises from sense experience" and making the O proposition read, "Some nontautological human knowledge does not arise from sense experience." Since I am seeking the simplest possible way of stating my point, I have decided to omit these and other qualifications that a more technical discussion would require. Any reader who wishes may simply add the qualification throughout the subsequent discussion. It should be understood, however, that it is by no means clear that the empiricist account of logical and mathematical truth as empty tautology is correct.

[2]See Augustine's *On The Trinity* 15. 12. 21., where he wrote, "Far be it from us to doubt the truth of what we have learned by the bodily senses."

the senses. That person is a rationalist (in *my* sense) who believes that *only one* item of human knowledge must have a nonsensory source. But the empiricist must be prepared to show how every thing human beings know has sense experience as its necessary and sufficient condition. As the history of philosophy makes clear, that is a rather formidable task.

THE TABULA RASA

Classical empiricists used to illustrate their basic claim that all human knowledge arises from sense experience by arguing that at birth the human mind is like a *tabula rasa*, a blank tablet. At birth, the human mind is like a totally clean blackboard; absolutely nothing is written on it. In other words, human beings are not born with any innate or inborn ideas or knowledge. The slate is clean. As the human being grows and develops, the senses supply the mind with an ever-increasing stock of information. All human knowledge results, on this model, from what the mind does with ideas supplied through the senses—the basic building blocks of knowledge.

Classical rationalists liked the model of the blank tablet because it gave them a convenient way of contrasting their own position with that of the empiricists. According to rationalism, the human mind is not a blank tablet at birth. On the contrary, the rationalists argued, if the human were not born with at least some inborn or innate ideas or categories or something, human knowledge about some things would be impossible; perhaps all human knowledge would be impossible.

This impotence of empiricism is especially evident in the case of human knowledge of universal and necessary truth. Brand Blanshard, perhaps the leading American rationalist of the twentieth century, has put this point well. According to Blanshard, reason "is the power and function of grasping necessary connections."[3] Many things in the world could have been otherwise. The typewriter I am using at this moment happens to be red; but it could have been blue. Whether it is red or not is a purely contingent feature of reality. Whatever color the typewriter happens to be, it could have been colored differently, But it is *necessarily* the case that my typewriter could not have been red all over and blue (or any other color) all over at the same time and in the same sense. The

---

[3]Brand Blanshard, *Reason and Analysis* (La Salle, Illinois: Open Court Publishing Co., 1962), p. 383.

necessary truth that my typewriter is red all over and not at the same time blue all over cannot be a function of sense experience. Sense experience may be able to report what is the case at a particular time. But sense experience is incapable of grasping what *must* be the case *at all times*. Sensation is impotent in the face of necessary and universal truth.

PLATO AND RATIONALISM

Plato made at least three important contributions to the rationalist tradition. First, he taught that all human knowledge contains an unavoidable reference to a universal element that is known a priori, that is, independently of sense experience. Secondly, Plato argued that reason is superior to sense perception because sensation is powerless to provide the crucial element present in all knowledge, namely, the universal and necessary. And finally, the superiority of reason over sense experience led Plato to think in terms of a hierarchy of epistemological states with reason at the top and sense perception at the bottom.

The Phaedo, one of Plato's dialogues, contains a passage that is especially helpful in clarifying the debate between rationalism and empiricism.[4] The passage is one in which Plato argues that all human knowledge arises out of preexistent knowledge. But this preexistent knowledge could not have been acquired through the senses since it is a necessary condition for anything that human beings can know. Plato has Socrates begin the argument by pointing out that people can only remember things they knew at some earlier time. Obviously, I cannot remember something in the present that I did not know previously. From this apparently innocent observation, he goes on to argue that some kind of remembering exists in every act of knowing. To illustrate his point, Plato uses judgments of the form, "a is equal to b." Consider a case where we judge that two sticks or two line segments are equal to each other. What must be the case before we can make the judgment that line a is equal to line b? Well, of course, we must have perceptual awareness of the two line segments. That is obvious. But, Plato insists, we must also have knowledge of something else which Plato calls The

---

[4]As a literary device, Plato puts the argument into the mouth of the imprisoned Socrates as he awaits his execution. No serious student of Plato thinks that the historical Socrates ever advanced this particular argument. The standard pagination for the *Phaedo* passage is 72e–77a.

Equal itself. That is, in addition to particular things like sticks or lines on a paper that we apprehend with our senses, there is something else, namely, the standard or idea or form of Equality, that must exist and be known before we can judge that the sticks or lines are equal. A person who did not know the essential nature of The Equal itself, would be incapable of making true judgments about equality, would never be able to judge that two line segments are equal in length or that two stones are equal in size.

But this raises the obvious question, where does our knowledge of the standard or form of Equality come from? How is this knowledge acquired? Plato gives two answers to this question, his own and one he rejects. It is interesting to note that the answer he rejects is the very position proposed later by his pupil Aristotle. It is the answer of classical empiricism. According to that view, human beings first perceive through their senses several things that are similar in a certain way. In this case, they are equal (for example, in size or length). From these several particulars, they then abstract an idea of the property or relation they share in common, namely, Equality. It should be easy to see how the position Plato rejects approximates the empiricist thesis that all human knowledge arises from sense experience: universals or forms like Equality can only be in the mind *after* particular examples are apprehended in sensible objects. Only then does the mind through abstraction or some other means grasp the universal.[5]

Plato offered two objections to what we have called the empiricist (or Aristotelian) theory that human beings come to know the eternal forms by abstracting a universal element from data supplied by the senses. First, Plato argued that it is absurd to believe that one first knows that a is equal to b, that c is equal to d, and then from these judgments about equal particulars, derive the more general knowledge of what Equality is. One could not know that a and b were equal to begin with unless he already knew the standard, The Equal itself. Knowledge of the universal is logically prior to knowledge of the particular. But since the awareness that a and b are equal is impossible without a logically prior knowledge of the form or universal (Equality), the empiricist thesis that

---

[5]No comfort can be found in the fact that Aristotle distinguished between a passive and active aspect of the human intellect. It is obvious that the Active Intellect mentioned in some of Aristotle's writings is useless until given sensible information to act upon.

all human knowledge arises from sense experience is false. Either the rationalist thesis that at least some human knowledge does not arise from sense experience is true or else no human knowledge is possible.

In his second objection, Plato argued that no particular thing or group of particular things is ever sufficient to provide a notion of the universal. Universals always have properties that can never be found in the earthly particulars that exemplify them. Particular things are always imperfect copies of the exemplars, the forms. It is impossible, for example, to obtain an idea of the perfect circle by contemplating examples of imperfect circles. Obviously, any circle that might be encountered in the physical world is imperfect. Since the concept of Equality could not possibly be derived from the senses and since we began to use these senses the moment we were born, our knowledge of The Equal itself must have been acquired independently of sense perception.[6]

I have explained the conflict between empiricism and rationalism in terms of their differing attitudes to the blank-tablet model of the mind. We then illustrated this disagreement through a study of an important passage in Plato's *Phaedo*. Another major difference between the two positions can be seen in their contrasting attitudes toward the Latin proposition, *Nihil est in intellectu nisi prius fuerit in sensu*: "Nothing is in the intellect which is not first in the senses." The rationalist Leibniz registered his disagreement with this empiricist thesis by adding four words: "except the intellect itself." *(Nihil est in intellectu quod no fuerit in sensu, excipe: nisi ipse intellectus.)*[7] As Leibniz explained, the differences between empiricists like John Locke and himself on such subjects is a matter of some importance. "The question is to know whether, following Aristotle and [Locke], the soul in itself is entirely empty, like a tablet on which nothing has yet been written *(tabula rasa)*, and whether all that is traced thereon comes solely from the senses and from experience; or whether as I, with Plato, believe, the soul contains originally the principles of several

---

[6]Plato of course went on to explain human a priori knowledge of the forms in terms of a theory of preexistence. Students of Plato differ as to whether Plato meant that theory to be taken literally or only offered it as a myth or likely story. For an account of how the mature Augustine modified Plato's position into his own theory of divine illumination, see Ronald Nash, "Some Philosophic Sources of Augustine's Illumination Theory," *Augustinian Studies* 2 (1971): 47–66.

[7]G. W. Leibniz, *New Essays in Human Understanding* 2. 1. 2.

notions and doctrines which external objects merely awaken on occasions."[8]

In the writings of rationalists like Descartes and Leibniz, rationalism came naturally to be associated with a belief in innate ideas. Unfortunately, their doctrine of innate ideas easily lent itself to caricature and misrepresentation, problems that plague rationalism to the present day. John Locke, for example, ridiculed a belief in innate ideas by pointing out that infants and many adults are in actuality unconscious of truths they are supposed to possess innately. Locke stacked the deck in his favor, however, by defining the word *idea* so that it only referred to something that was an actual object of consciousness.

Descartes had used the word *idea* in a quite different way to denote something that was a *possible* object of thought or consciousness. The innate ideas that Descartes and Leibniz were concerned to defend were known *implicitly*. In the words of Leibniz, "What is innate is not at first known clearly and distinctly as such; often much attention and method is necessary in order to perceive it. Students do not always do so, still less every human being."[9] As Frederick Copleston explains, "To say that the idea of God is innate thus means for Leibniz, as it meant for Descartes, that the mind can arrive at this idea from within and that by internal reflection alone it can come to know the truth of the proposition that God exists."[10]

With this background, we can now turn our attention to the nature of rationalism and the topic of innate ideas in the Christian philosophy of St. Augustine.[11]

---

[8]Ibid., preface, paragraph 3.

[9]Ibid., 1. 2. 12.

[10]Frederick Copleston, A *History of Philosophy*, 9 vols. (Westminster, Maryland: The Newman Press, 1961), 4: 319. Copleston's comments about Descartes' use of the phrase *innate ideas* should also be noted. He writes that "for Descartes, innate ideas are *a priori* forms of thought which are not really distinct from the faculty of thinking. Axioms such as those mentioned above are not present in the mind as objects of thought from the beginning; but they are virtually present in the sense that by reason of its innate constitution the mind thinks in these ways. Descartes' theory would thus constitute to some extent an anticipation of Kant's theory of the *a priori*, with the important difference that Descartes does not say, and indeed does not believe, that the *a priori* forms of thought are applicable only within the field of sense experience." Ibid., p. 83.

[11]A discussion of the varied expressions of contemporary rationalism and empiricism in America would obviously exceed the bounds of this book. I will therefore limit myself to a few bibliographic comments. Many would agree that the most important American exponent of rationalism in the twentieth century has been Brand Blanshard. His huge

work, *Reason and Analysis* (La Salle, Illinois: Open Court Publishing Co., 1961) contains a major defense of the basic concerns of rationalism. It should be noted in passing, however, that Gordon Clark maintains that Blanshard ultimately makes too many concessions to empiricism. Most of Blanshard's criticisms of empiricism are directed against Logical Positivism and its successors in the English-speaking world. It is unfortunate that Blanshard did not give more attention to the views of Willard Van Orman Quine who is widely perceived as the dominant empiricist on the contemporary scene. Quine's position can be surveyed in his *From a Logical Point of View* (Cambridge, Mass.: Harvard University Press, 1953). A readable introduction to Quine's philosophy is Alex Orenstein's *Willard Van Orman Quine* (Boston: Twayne Publishers, 1977). Another readable work that serves as an introduction to Quinean neo-Pragmatism is Bruce Aune's *Rationalism, Empiricism and Pragmatism* (New York: Random House, 1970). Articles that represent the kind of criticism I would offer of Quine and neo-Pragmatism include the following: Henry Veatch, "Logical Truth," *Journal of Philosophy* (1956), pp. 671–79; Henry Veatch, "Is Quine a Metaphysician?" *The Review of Metaphysics* (1978), pp. 406–30; Michael Dummett, "Is Logic Empirical?" in *Contemporary British Philosophy*, 4th Series, ed. H. D. Lewis (London: George Allen & Unwin, 1976), pp. 45–68; and Carl R. Kordig, "Some Statements Are Immune to Revision," *The New Scholasticism* (1981), pp. 69–76. One factor that complicates the present debate is the tendency of some contemporary rationalists like Alvin Plantinga to shift the discussion to the subject of essence. See Plantinga's *The Nature of Necessity* (New York: Oxford University Press, 1974).

Chapter 8

The Christian Rationalism of St. Augustine

Our goal, remember, is an answer to the question: Can the human mind know the mind of God? I have suggested that an affirmative answer to that question flows reasonably and naturally from the early church's conviction that Jesus Christ is the divine Logos which lightens every human mind and makes human knowledge possible, a view that has important affinities with certain elements in the rationalist tradition in Western philosophy. In chapter 7, I attempted to explain the fundamental differences between rationalism and empiricism. Empiricists believe that all human knowledge can be accounted for on the basis of prior sense experience. As I use the term, rationalists believe that human beings know at least some things that cannot be explained in this way. Rationalists like Descartes and Leibniz found it useful to account for such knowledge in terms of innate ideas. These innate ideas were understood by thinkers like Descartes and Leibniz to be dispositions or aptitudes to think in certain ways.

I will now attempt to trace some of these same elements of rationalism in the thought of St. Augustine. Augustine eventually introduced some rather significant modifications into Plato's account of knowledge, adjustments in which Augustine took an innatist position. For Augustine, the innate ideas which are a necessary condition for human knowledge are explained in terms of a theory of divine illumination. This chapter's examination of Augustine's theory of knowledge and its relationship to the views of Plato will help make clear some important implications of our earlier discussion of the Christian Logos doctrine.

DIVINE ILLUMINATION

There has been a long and as yet unresolved controversy over the meaning of Augustine's theory of divine illumination. The divine light is Augustine's answer to how humans know the eternal ideas that subsist in the mind of God. Since Augustine believed that a knowledge of the Forms is a necessary condition for any knowledge of temporal reality, all human knowledge must be explained ultimately in terms of the divine light. Unfortunately, there is no generally accepted interpretation of Augustine's illumination theory.

My own contribution to the controversy over how Augustine's theory of the divine light should be interpreted is *The Light of the Mind: St. Augustine's Theory of Knowledge.*[1] In it I argue that some of the most commonly accepted interpretations of Augustine's illumination theory must be rejected. This includes the attempt of Father Charles Boyer[2] and others to revive the theory of St. Thomas Aquinas, an attempt that has the effect of turning the flaming rationalist Augustine into a crypto-empiricist.[3] Attempting to force a theory of abstraction into Augustine's theory of knowledge, these interpreters tended to scholasticize Augustine to the exclusion of his Platonism. It is also necessary to reject Etienne Gilson's interpretation.[4] As Gilson saw it, the nature of God's illuminating activity is purely formal. That is, the function of illumination is not to give the human mind some definite content of knowledge of the Forms, but simply to convey the quality of certainty and necessity to certain judgments. Gilson was correct in what he affirmed but wrong in what he denied. My book discusses a number of texts from Augustine's writings that make it clear that he meant his theory of divine illumination to explain not only the quality but also the content of necessary truths.[5] Gilson's view leaves Augustine without any answer to the crucial question of how we come to know the Forms.

The interpretation I advanced suggests that any adequate understanding of Augustine's theory of illumination must take account of the

[1]Ronald Nash, *The Light of the Mind: St. Augustine's Theory of Knowledge* (Lexington: University of Kentucky Press, 1969).
[2]C. Boyer, *L'Idée de vérité dans la philosophie de saint Augustin* (Paris, 1921).
[3]For my criticisms of this position, see *The Light of the Mind*, pp. 94–97.
[4]Etienne Gilson, *The Christian Philosophy of Saint Augustine* (New York: Random House, 1960), pp. 79, 86, 91.
[5]See *The Light of the Mind*, pp. 109–11.

fact that two lights are involved in any act of human knowledge. Augustine is very careful in *Against Faustus, the Manichaean* to distinguish between the uncreated light of God and a different, created light, namely, the human mind, which plays a necessary role in knowledge.[6] In other words, human knowledge is made possible by two lights, the uncreated light of God and the created, mutable light which is human intellect. Just as the moon derives the light it reflects from the sun, so the rational human mind derives a created ability to know from its origin, God. Human knowledge can be regarded as a reflection of the truth originating in the mind of God. To be more specific, God has endowed humans with a structure of rationality patterned after the divine ideas in His own mind: we can know truth because God has made us like Himself. This helps explain how we can know not only the eternal Forms but also the creation that is patterned after these Forms. We can know the corporeal world because we first know and understand the intelligible world. As an inherent part of our rational nature, we possess forms of thought by which we know and judge sensible things. Because God has created humankind after His own image and continually sustains and aids the soul in its quest for knowledge, human knowledge is possible. God is the original source of the light that makes knowledge possible because He is the reason or logos of the universe. All the truths of reason have their ground in His very being; they subsist in His own mind. Because humankind was created in the image of God, the human mind is a secondary and derivative source of light that reflects in a creaturely way the rationality of the Creator. A harmony or correlation exists therefore between the mind of God, the human mind, and the rational structure of the world.

THE ETERNAL REASONS

Augustine accepted Plato's view that in addition to the earthly, corporeal, and temporal world of particular things (like trees, rocks, birds, and so on) apprehended through the senses, there exists another world that is incorporeal and nontemporal. This latter world of Forms or Ideas[7] serves as an archetype or model of created reality. What Plato

---

[6]*Against Faustus, the Manichaean* 20, 7.
[7]Examples of such Forms include absolute Beauty, Truth, and Goodness along with the concepts of such things as numbers, the square, the circle, and so on.

called Forms or Ideas, Augustine called *rationes aeternae*, the eternal reasons. Augustine regarded them as

> principle forms or stable and unchangeable essences of things. They are themselves not formed, and they are eternal and always in the same state because they are contained in God's intelligence. They neither come into being nor do they pass away, but everything that can or does come into being and pass away is formed in accordance with them.[8]

Like Plato, Augustine argued that before an architect builds an edifice, he must first have a model of what he intends to build. Similarly, God had a plan before He created the universe. His creation is patterned after the divine ideas. Because the eternal reasons are the exemplary cause of everything that exists in the physical universe, they are the basic foundation of all created reality. Moreover, because the judgments humans make must accord with the eternal forms, they are a necessary condition for human knowledge. Plato did not make clear the precise relationship between the forms and his god. Augustine eliminated this lacuna in Plato's system and regarded the forms as eternal, immutable truths subsisting in the mind of God. Since the forms are ideas that subsist in the mind of God, they share God's attributes of eternity, necessity, and immutability.

St. Augustine was clearly aware that his own Christian theory of knowledge had roots in the New Testament Logos doctrine. He was just as conscious of the debt he owed to the Platonic epistemology he inherited from the neo-Platonists he had studied. In Book 10 of his *City of God*, Augustine credited Plotinus as one of the sources of his theory of illumination and suggested that Plotinus' discussion of the role of light in human knowledge had affinities to St. John's comments about the light of God in the prologue to the fourth Gospel (the same text, of course, that contains John's teaching about the Logos). John's account, Augustine wrote, "shows that a rational or intellectual soul . . . cannot be a light to itself but needs to be illumined by participation in the true Light. This is what John himself confesses in his witness to the Word."[9]

Augustine's theory of divine illumination was his answer to the question: How does the human mind come to know the eternal forms

---

[8] Augustine, *On Various Questions* 46, 1–2.
[9] *The City of God* 10, 2.

that subsist in the mind of God? As a first step towards understanding Augustine's illumination theory, it is important to recognize three possible answers that he rejected. For Augustine, a human being does not acquire knowledge of the forms by sense experience, by Platonic recollection, or by teaching.

Augustine's rejection of sense experience as the source of human knowledge of universal truth is similar to Plato's position in *The Phaedo*. Just as Plato taught that every judgment about equal things presupposes a prior knowledge of Equality, Augustine argued that all judgments about number presuppose a prior knowledge of Unity. But the notion of Unity cannot be derived from experience. "Whoever thinks with exactitude of unity will discover that it cannot be perceived by the senses. Whatever comes into contact with a bodily sense is proved to be not one but many, for it is corporeal and therefore has innumerable parts."[10] The senses bring a person into contact only with corporeal things. But no corporeal object is a true example of Unity. Therefore, human knowledge of Unity must come not from the senses but through divine illumination. As Augustine wrote elsewhere, "True equality and similitude, true and primal unity, are not perceived by the eye of the flesh or by any bodily sense, but are known by the mind."[11] For Augustine, knowledge of the forms is independent of sense experience.

But while Augustine followed Plato in rejecting sense experience as a ground for human knowledge of the forms, his mature position rejected Plato's own appeal to the preexistence of the soul and recollection. True, during the first few years after his conversion (A.D. 387–389), the young Augustine believed in the preexistence of the soul and accepted Plato's explanation of human knowledge in terms of recollection.[12] As Augustine's thought matured and he came to see the unbiblical implications of the doctrine of preexistence, he sought a different answer for the problem of how one comes to know the forms.[13] He

[10]Augustine, *On the Freedom of the Will* 2, 8, 22.

[11]Augustine, *On True Religion* 30, 55.

[12]For a discussion of Augustine's early commitment to preexistence and the theory of recollection, see Etienne Gilson, *The Christian Philosophy of Saint Augustine* (New York: Random House, 1960), pp. 71–72. Compare also the following texts in Augustine: *Against the Skeptics* 2, 9, 22 with *Retractions* 1, 1, 3; *Soliloquies* 2, 20, 35 with *Retractions* 1, 4, 4; and *On the Measure of the Soul* 20, 34 with *Retractions* 1, 8.

[13]Augustine leaves absolutely no doubt concerning his final rejection of Platonic recollection in *On The Trinity* 12, 15, 24.

continued to believe that all human knowledge presupposes a prior knowledge of the forms and that these forms cannot be known through the senses. But he came to hold that God has implanted a knowledge of the forms in the human mind contemporaneous with birth. In other words, Augustine's account of human knowledge replaced Plato's appeal to recollection with a theory of innate ideas that belong to humankind by virtue of our creation in the image of God.

Finally, Augustine rejects the view that human knowledge of the eternal forms might be acquired through teaching. The writing in which Augustine states this argument, On The Teacher, is complex and thus easy to misunderstand. But his conclusion is clear: knowledge of a priori truth cannot be passed from one person to another as through teaching. It must always arise within the soul. "Concerning universals of which we can have knowledge, we do not listen to anyone speaking and making sounds outside ourselves. We listen to Truth which presides over our minds within us, though of course we may be bidden to listen by someone using words. Our real Teacher is he who is so listened to, who is said to dwell in the inner man, namely, Christ, that is, the unchangeable power and eternal wisdom of God."[14] While Augustine's language sounds mystical, his point is philosophical. Every human knows the forms because God endows him or her with this knowledge and continually sustains the intellect in the knowing process. The true teacher is Christ, who Himself is the truth and who, in the words of the fourth Gospel, "lighteth every man that cometh into the world."

But if a person cannot come to know the eternal forms through experience, through Platonic recollection, or through teaching, how can they be known? Augustine: by divine illumination. But what did Augustine mean by his appeal to the divine light?

THREE PARADOXES

Any adequate account of Augustine's theory of knowledge in general and of his doctrine of illumination in particular must deal satisfactorily with three paradoxes in his thought. First, Augustine seems to teach that the human intellect is both active and passive. Second, he teaches that the forms are distinct from and not distinct from the human

---

[14]Augustine, On The Teacher, 11.

mind. Third, he writes that the human mind is and is not the light that makes knowledge possible.

(1) *The human intellect is both passive and active with regard to the forms.*

Augustine says that the law of God has been transcribed on the human soul.[15] In *One the Trinity*, he affirms that the rules by which humans make moral judgments are impressed on our heart as a seal is impressed on wax.[16] Just as a person does not create the sensible objects he or she experiences (they are just given), so humans do not create the eternal forms. They are *given* and we must accommodate our judgment to them. But humans do not simply receive a knowledge of the forms. Knowledge (*scientia*) is possible only because each person can use these eternal standards of judgment by bringing them to bear upon sense images. Animals can perceive corporeal things through the bodily senses and store images of these things in their memory. However, the beast cannot relate these perceptions and memory images to truth or the eternal standards, as a person can. Augustine once wrote that when he recalled a beautiful stone arch at Carthage, there was more in his mind than simply an image of that arch. "I behold in my mind yet another thing, according to which that work of art pleases me; and whence also, if it displeased me, I should correct it. We judge therefore of those particular things according to that [form of eternal truth] and discern that form by the intuition of the rational mind."[17] Thus for Augustine, human knowledge of sensible things is more than mere sensation. It is an active relating of the thing sensed to eternal standards, the forms. The mind clearly plays an active role in knowledge.

(2) *The forms are and are not separate from the human mind.*

First of all, Augustine teaches that the forms are and indeed must be distinct from the human intellect. In *On the Trinity* he speaks of the forms as "above the eye of the mind."[18] One of the important arguments of *On the Freedom of the Will* is that truth is superior to the

---

[15]*On Order*, 1, 8, 25.

[16]*On the Trinity* 14, 15, 21.

[17]*On the Trinity* 9, 6, 10, tr. A. W. Hadden and W. G. T. Shedd in *Basic Writings of St. Augustine* (New York: Random House, 1948).

[18]Ibid., 2, 6, 11.

human mind.[19] Again in *On the Trinity* he explains that unless the forms "were above the human mind, [they] would certainly not be unchangeable."[20] If the eternal reasons are not distinct from the human mind, they will suffer from the same mutability and finiteness that characterize human reason. The same passage adds, however, that "unless something of our own [mind] were subjoined to them [the forms], we should not be able to employ them as our measures by which to judge of corporeal things."

Many passages in Augustine's writings suggest that the forms are part of the rational nature of humanity. In his *Confessions* Augustine writes, "The memory contains also the reasons and innumerable laws of numbers and dimensions, none of which has any sense of the body impressed."[21] In *On the Immortality of the Soul*, he teaches that "when we reason with ourselves or some other person asks us skillful questions, we discover truth in our minds."[22] Later in the same work he comments, "Those things that are comprehended by the intellect, however, are comprehended as existing nowhere else but in the comprehending mind itself, and, at the same time, as not contained in space."[23] He asks how we could see that some things are good and better than other things "unless a conception of the good itself had been impressed upon us, such that according to it we might both approve some things as good and prefer one good to another."[24]

One of the most important passages in this connection is found in the eighth book of *The City of God:* "For there is no corporeal beauty, whether in the condition of a body, as figure, or in its movement, as in music, of which it is not the mind that judges. But this could never have been, had there not existed *in the mind itself* a superior form of these things, without bulk, without noise of voice, without space and time."[25] This passage states something more than that the forms must be related to the mind. It states specifically that the mind could not judge unless these ideas actually existed in the mind. But the presence of these forms

---

[19]*On the Freedom of the Will* 2, 15, 39.
[20]*On the Trinity* 12, 2, 2.
[21]*Confessions* 10, 12.
[22]*On the Immortality of the Soul* 4.
[23]Ibid., 6.
[24]*On the Trinity* 8, 3, 4.
[25]*The City of God* 8, 6.

in the mind, he continues, does not make the mind immutable. "But even in respect of these things, had the mind not been mutable, it would not have been possible for one to judge better than another with regard to sensible forms. He who is clever judges better than he who is slow, he who is skilled than he who is unskilled, he who is practiced than he who is unpracticed; and the same person judges better after he has gained experience than he did before."[26]

In keeping with the rationalist insistence that innate ideas exist within the mind implicitly or virtually, Augustine held that the laws of mathematics along with the eternal forms are present in the human mind as latent or virtual truth. Even when they are not present as objects of conscious thought, they are in the mind as predispositions of the mind to think in certain ways. Human knowledge of the forms involves an actualization of latent or virtual knowledge stored in the mind.

In Augustine's system then the forms exist in three distinct but related modes.[27] The first is the form that appears as the eternal archetype subsisting in the mind of God. The second is the form particular things possess by virtue of their creation after the eternal pattern. And finally, there is the sense in which forms exist in the human mind.

(3) *The human mind is and is not a light that makes knowledge possible.*

Augustine asserts that the light that makes knowledge possible does not designate human reason. "The light of minds is above minds and surpasses all minds."[28] In *Against Faustus, The Manichaean*, however, Augustine teaches that there is a sense in which the changeable and finite human mind *is* a light.[29] This passage resolves the paradox about whether or not the human mind is the light that makes knowledge possible by suggesting that there are actually two lights that make knowledge possible—the uncreated Light of God and the created, mutable light, which is human intellect. Just as the moon derives the light it reflects from the sun, so the rational human mind derives a created

---

[26]Ibid.
[27]See *The City of God* 8, 6.
[28]*On the Gospel According to John* 3, 4.
[29]*Against Faustus, The Manichaean* 20, 7.

ability to know from its origin, God. Human knowledge can be regarded as a reflection of the truth originating in the mind of God. But the human mind and knowledge are in one important respect perfectly natural (as opposed to supernatural), since the knowledge is derived from rational capacities that are an *inherent* part of human nature.

A synthesis of Augustine's three paradoxes of knowledge leads unavoidably to the following conclusion: The forms or eternal ideas in the human mind are a priori, virtual preconditions of knowledge. They are to use Kant's term, a priori because they cannot be derived from experience. They are virtual because they are said to be in the mind or memory even when they are not objects of thought.[30] Finally, the forms are preconditions of knowledge because knowledge becomes possible only when these universals are applied to images from sensation.

Augustine can speak of the mind as a created light because he believes that the forms have been put there in some sense. In *On the Freedom of the Will*, Augustine writes that the laws by which we judge beauty are in the mind. "You will return to your mind within, and know that you could neither approve nor disapprove things of sense unless you had within you, as it were, laws of beauty by which you judge all beautiful things which you perceive in the world."[31] This is also true in the case of goodness itself. We would be unable to make value judgments "unless a conception (*notio*) of the good itself had been impressed upon us."[32]

God has endowed humans with a structure of rationality patterned after the divine ideas in His own mind.[33] We can know truth because God has made us like Himself. If this claim is true, it helps to explain how the human mind can know not only the eternal forms but also the creation that is patterned after these forms. We can know the corporeal world only because we first know and understand the intelligible world. Forms of thought by which we know and judge sensible things are an

---

[30]*On the Immortality of the Soul* 4.
[31]*On the Freedom of the Will* 2, 16, 41.
[32]*On the Trinity* 8, 3, 4.
[33]This position is sometimes called *The Preformation Theory*. For more on the similarities and differences between this view and Kant's theory of knowledge, see the following: Ronald H. Nash, ed., *The Philosophy of Gordon H. Clark* (Philadelphia: Presbyterian and Reformed, 1969), pp. 141ff.; Gordon Clark, *Thales to Dewey* (Grand Rapids: Baker, 1981), pp. 410–11; and Gordon Clark, *A Christian View of Men and Things* (Grand Rapids: Eerdmans, 1951), pp. 312–18.

inherent part of our natures. I concur with Richard Ackworth, who writes:

> St. Augustine's view seems to have been that these *a priori* standards or *notiones impressae* are originally virtual or nonconscious and of the nature of predispositions to recognize, for instance, imperfect goodness in the light of perfect goodness; we come consciously to know them only by reflecting on the judgments made in their light. But the *notio* of goodness is not abstracted from the objects judged to be good, for it had to be virtually present *a priori* for us to be able to recognize them as good at all.[34]

Augustine's three paradoxes are easily resolved. Whether the mind is or is not a light that makes knowledge possible is resolved when one sees that there are really two lights—the created, intelligible light that is the human mind and the uncreated, intelligible light that is God. Concerning the relation of the forms to mind, we have seen that the forms exist first (temporally, logically, and ontologically) in the mind of God and exist in a derived form in the rational structure of the human mind. Whether the human mind is active or passive may be the easiest to resolve: It is largely passive with regard to universals (although rational powers sharpen understanding of these ideas) and active with regard to knowledge (*scientia*) of corporeal things known through the senses. The mind is active in *scientia* because sensible things must be judged according to the standards of the universals.

To know truth, the mind is necessary, but not sufficient. According to Augustine, the created light of human intellect needs a light from without.[35] Even the created intelligible light would be unable to account for human knowledge without the constant, immanent, and active presence of God.[36] We must not think of the forms as having been given to humans once-and-for-all. Though the forms are part of the rational structure of the human mind and belong there by virtue of our having been created in the image of God, the soul never ceases to be dependent upon God for its knowledge. B. B. Warfield, commenting on Augustine,

---

[34]Richard Ackworth, "God and Human Knowledge," *The Downside Review*, 75 (1957): 108–9.

[35]*On the Position of the Pelagians* 3, 7.

[36]*On Genesis* 7, 31, 59.

says: "God, having so made man, has not left him deistically, to himself, but continually reflects into his soul the contents of His truths which constitute the intelligible world. The soul is therefore in unbroken communion with God, and in the body of intelligible truths reflected into it from God, sees God."[37] Thus, knowledge is possible because God has created each person after His own image as a rational soul and because God continually sustains and aids the soul in its quest for knowledge.

To summarize: The forms or eternal ideas exist in the mind of God (independently of particular things), but in a secondary sense they also exist in the human mind. God created humans with a structure of rationality patterned after the divine forms in His own mind. This innate knowledge is part of what it means to be created in the image of God. In addition to knowledge of forms, knowledge of the world is possible because God has also patterned the world after the divine ideas. We can know the corporeal world because God has given man a knowledge of these ideas by which we can judge sensations and gain knowledge.

I regard these conclusions as merely an elaboration or logical extension of the Logos doctrine. Augustine is one Christian theist who believed that the claim that the human logos is part of the image of God rests on a sound philosophical and theological ground. He believed that the Logos teaching of the New Testament and the early church fathers entailed a similarity between the rational structure of the human mind and the rational structure of the divine mind. It is possible for the human logos to know the divine Logos because God created the human being as a creature who has the God-given ability to know the divine mind and to think God's thoughts after Him. The laws of reason are the same for both God and humans.[38]

---

[37]B. B. Warfield, *Calvin and Augustine* (Philadelphia: Presbyterian and Reformed, 1956), p. 397.

[38]The positions we have taken in chapters 7 and 8 will raise two questions for some readers. (1) Some Roman Catholics will be troubled that our interpretation of St. Augustine entails that a saint of the church held a view (namely, Ontologism) that the church has condemned as a heresy. I discuss the ramifications of this problem in chapter 8 of *The Light of the Mind: St. Augustine's Theory of Knowledge*. See also E. J. Carnell, *An Introduction to Christian Apologetics* (Grand Rapids: Eerdmans, 1948), pp. 152ff. (2) Christian empiricists insist that all human knowledge of God is analogical by which they mean that no human language can have the same (univocal) meaning applied to God that it has when applied to sensible things. My position obviously entails the denial of this view. For more on the subject, see *The Philosophy of Gordon H. Clark*, pp. 149ff. or Carnell, *Apologetics*, pp. 140ff.

Chapter 9

The Religious Revolt Against Logic

In chapter 5, I suggested that the alternative to theological scepticism that I seek requires that I explain and relate several topics. I must first explain the Logos doctrine of early Christian thought and show how a Christian theory of knowledge can evolve from that view. St. Augustine's theory of knowledge was used as an example of one way this development might occur. Second, I must explain the differences between rationalism and empiricism, and relate my position to the former. Third, I must present a theory about the law of noncontradiction that will counter the tendency of so many modern theologians to contrast human logic to divine logic. Chapters 6, 7, and 8 contain my attempt to accomplish the first two goals. Along the way I have attempted to show that the kind of position I recommend has a long and an honored tradition. By now, an outline of the position I will take on the third point should be coming into view.

Throughout the discussion thus far, repeated use has been made of the word *reason*. The word obviously has had several meanings in the history of philosophy. Thomas Aquinas used it in contrast with special revelation; David Hume on the other hand contrasted reason with experience. For my position, *reason* means logic, the forms of thought, the laws of valid inference.

One highly visible feature of much contemporary religious thought is a pervasive spirit of misology, a hatred of logic. In this connection, recall some of the words of W. T. Stace that were quoted in the introduction: "God is utterly and forever beyond the reach of the logical intellect or of any intellectual comprehension, and that in consequence when we try to comprehend his nature intellectually, contradictions appear in our thinking."[1] The astute reader will now recognize Stace's position for what it is, a modern restatement of Kantian scepticism about God dressed up as mysticism. Stace insists that "any attempt to reach God through logic, through the conceptual, logical intellect, is doomed."[2]

Stace resisted all efforts to remove elements of contradiction in utterances about God. He chided other mystics in particular for yielding to their rational impulses and seeking ways to eliminate contradictions in their thinking about God. The proper course, he suggested, was to glory in the contradictions.

> My own belief is that all attempts to rationalize the paradox, to make it logically acceptable, are futile because the paradoxes of religion and of mysticism are irresoluble by the human intellect. My view is that they never have been, they never can be, and they never will be resolved, or made logical. . . . When you say that God is incomprehensible, one thing you mean is just that these contradictions break out in our intellect and cannot be resolved, no matter how clever or how good a logician you may be.[3]

Stace especially criticized Buddhist mystics who attempt to remove contradictions in their system by postulating two Brahmans, a higher and lower. "One may be quite sure," Stace advised, "that this is the wrong solution because the religious intuition is preemptory that God is one and not two."[4] Logic then simply does not apply in religion. Stace was not simply saying that religion could be unreasonable in the sense that it discussed things that were above human reason. Religion was actually against logic. "Should we say that there is contradiction in the nature of God himself, in the ultimate being? Well, if we were to say that, I think that we shouldn't be saying anything very unusual or very shocking."[5] It should come as no surprise that I regard my own position as the antithesis of Stace's view.

---

[1]Stace, p. 19.
[2]Ibid., p. 20.
[3]Ibid., p. 17.
[4]Ibid.
[5]Ibid., pp. 18–19.

But if Stace were correct and logic has no relevance to the kind of mysticism he represented, it is difficult to understand most of what he wrote. For example, why, given his repudiation of logic, did he criticize those Buddhists who rejected the unity of God in favor of two Brahmans? Once logic is disavowed, God can be both one *and* two (or two thousand) at the same time and in the same sense. If a distinction can be drawn between a monistic God and a dualistic or pluralistic deity, then logic must have some relevance after all. Once logic is denied, inconsistency becomes a virtue.

KIERKEGAARD, BRUNNER, BARTH, AND TORRANCE

But since Stace was a mystic (and a non-Christian mystic, at that), his enthusiasm for irrationalism may lack some relevance for a study of Christian thinking on the subject of God and logic. Can a similar distrust for or contempt for logic and reason be found in the writings of Christian theologians? One thing that hinders a simple answer to this question is that few writers are as daring and as explicit as Stace. Discussions about the proper place of reason in religion are frequently plagued by inattention to two quite different senses the word *reason* can have. Consider the following claims:

(1) The Incarnation is unreasonable; that is, the claim that Jesus Christ is God is incredible. I simply cannot believe it.

(2) The Incarnation is unreasonable; that is, the doctrine of the Incarnation violates the law of noncontradiction.

In the second case, a particular Christian belief allegedly violates a principle or law of logic. Anything that is unreasonable or irrational in sense (2) is such in an objective and universal way. But in the first case, a particular Christian belief is called unreasonable simply because some person cannot understand it or believe it. Unreasonableness in sense (1) is person-relative. It should be obvious that all sorts of beliefs that some people cannot accept and thus find irrational are readily acceptable and rational to others.

When religious thinkers like Søren Kierkegaard, Karl Barth, and Emil Brunner proclaimed the irrationality of certain Christian beliefs, I suspect that what they really meant to say was that something about

Christianity was so shocking and so offensive to the "reason" of many unbelievers that they (the unbelievers) found it irrational. Since the New Testament itself suggests this position, and since it accords with what any observer can detect in the reactions of people to many Christian claims, the view itself is quite unexceptionable.

Unfortunately, the extreme rhetoric of some Christian writers suggests that they also mean to say that Christianity is unreasonable in the second sense, that it actually involves violations of the law of non-contradiction. The writings of the Scottish disciple of Karl Barth, Thomas Torrance, are a case in point. Torrance certainly appears to claim that there is a difference between God's logic and human logic, and, further, that the forms of "human logic" cannot be extended to a transcendent God.[6] Torrance seems to believe that human logic, human reasoning, human concepts, and human language are all inadequate to a knowledge of the Christian God. He writes that human "ideas and conceptions and analogies and words are too limited and narrow and poor for knowledge of God."[7] His suspicions about purely "human" logic are evident in such statements as: "Real theological thinking" should be freed from "imprisonment in timeless logical connections."[8] Knowledge of *eternal* truth, he suggests, is hindered by insisting on "fixed categories of thought."[9] What Torrance seems to give us is a statement that human knowledge about God is impossible and that human forms of reasoning are completely incapable of understanding truth and reason as it exists in the mind of God.

Several objections quickly come to mind. For one thing, if the principles of logic are as tentative and mutable as Torrance suggests, how can any reader have any confidence in the validity of Torrance's own reasoning? If God Himself cannot reveal timeless truths or universally valid information to us, what leads Torrance to think that he can? His book purports to be true and to contain universally valid information. How then can Torrance do something that God cannot? Carl F. H. Henry notes, in utter amazement, that in all of his contentions,

---

[6]See Thomas F. Torrance, *Theological Science* (London: Oxford University Press, 1969), pp. 54, 153, 205, and other passages.

[7]Ibid., p. 49.

[8]Ibid., p. 54.

[9]Ibid., p. 153.

Torrance seems to be privy to objective propositional knowledge about God which his methodology pointedly disallows to other human beings. From what source, for example, did Torrance derive the information that "there is an ultimate objectivity which cannot be enclosed within the creaturely objectivities through which we encounter it, an objectivity that "indefinitely transcends' creaturely objectivities."[10]

Torrance's repeated use of assumptions he denies to others does not speak well of his consistency. As Henry goes on to point out, Torrance's position reduces to scepticism:

The insistence on a logical gulf between human conceptions and God as the object of religious knowledge is erosive of knowledge and cannot escape a reduction to skepticism. Concepts that by definition are inadequate to the truth of God cannot be made to compensate for logical deficiency by appealing either to God's omnipotence or to his grace. Nor will it do to call for a restructuring of logic in the interest of knowledge of God. Whoever calls for a higher logic must preserve the existing laws of logic to escape pleading the cause of illogical nonsense.[11]

If a transcendent God really does have a logic all His own, no criteria can exist in the realm of the transcendent to distinguish between Yahweh and Satan. "If the law of contradiction is irrelevant in the sphere of transcendent ontology, then God and the not-God, the divine and the demonic, cannot be assuredly differentiated."[12] Finally, Henry objects, "Torrance's disavowal of authentic knowledge of God does not characterize the biblical prophets and apostles, far less Jesus of Nazareth; rather, it reflects the dialectical epistemology to which unfortunately much of twentieth-century religious theory is indebted."[13]

DONALD BLOESCH

The contemporary distrust of logic has found a home within Evangelicalism. Donald Bloesch, a well-known evangelical theologian,

---

[10]Carl Henry, *God, Revelation and Authority*, 3: 223.
[11]Ibid., 3: 229.
[12]Ibid., 2: 60.
[13]Ibid., 3: 214.

levels his own attack against reason. Bloesch takes issue with the belief "that man's logic and knowledge are identical with God's."[14] If Bloesch means to say that Christianity is irrational in the sense that it violates the law of noncontradiction, his view leads to absurdity. If God possesses knowledge and humans possess something entirely different, then whatever is attained, it cannot be knowledge. If there is absolutely no point of contact between the divine logic and a so-called human logic, then what passes as human "reasoning" can never be valid. And, of course, if this were so, then the putative reasoning in Bloesch's own book would be invalid.

HERMAN DOOYEWEERD

One of the most surprising reappearances of Hume's Gap in recent thought is found in the philosophy of the Dutch Calvinist, Herman Dooyeweerd. Dooyeweerd's system[15] is central to the thought of a small team of Calvinist thinkers who form the faculty of the Institute for Christian Studies in Toronto, Canada.[16] It is not necessary to go into the details of Dooyeweerd's philosophy.[17] What is important for our present purposes is Dooyeweerd's theory of "The Boundary." The doctrine of the Boundary is the most important way followers of Dooyeweerd emphasize the sovereignty and transcendence of God. All of God's creation is subject to various laws such as the laws of physics, the laws of biology, the laws of mathematics, the laws of thinking, the laws of economics, and so on. Because God is the Lawgiver, He Himself is not subject to the laws that govern His creation. Law then constitutes a

---

[14]Donald Bloesch, *Essentials of Evangelical Theology*, 2 vols. (San Francisco: Harper and Row, 1978), 1: 75.

[15]Dooyeweerd's system is known by several names including The Philosophy of the Cosmonomic Idea and The Amsterdam Philosophy.

[16]The Toronto-based Institute for Christian Studies should not be confused with The Institute for Advanced Christian Studies, a rotating board of eight evangelical academicians that supports Christian scholarship. At various times, this board has included Carl F. H. Henry, Kenneth Kantzer, John Snyder, Arthur Holmes, John Scanzoni, V. Elving Anderson, Charles Hatfield, Robert Frykenberg, Ronald Nash, James Packer, C. Everett Koop, and others.

[17]I did this myself to some extent in a book entitled *Dooyeweerd and the Amsterdam Philosophy* (Grand Rapids: Zondervan, 1962). That book was the work of a very young man and were he to do much writing on the subject now, his treatment would be much more critical. A more recent and more sympathetic portrayal of Dooyeweerd's philosophy is L. Kalsbeek's *Contours of a Christian Philosophy* (Toronto: Wedge, 1975). Both books contain helpful bibliographies.

boundary between God and the cosmos. The laws that apply *under* the Boundary do not apply to God who is above all Law.

Few Christians, prior to their recognition of the implications of the theory, would dispute the suggestion that a boundary exists between God and His creation. The doctrine seems innocent enough until one realizes how the Dooyeweerdians apply the theory to human reason. In their hands, what should have been a helpful metaphor is interpreted in the most literal terms so as to exclude totally the Logos doctrine. For the followers of Dooyeweerd, the laws of logic, of valid inference, exist *only* on man's side of the Boundary. L. Kalsbeek makes clear the gap or wall that Dooyeweerdians think exists between the mind of God and the human mind:

> With our human thinking and the laws established for it, we find ourselves on the creaturely side of that boundary, unable to cross it because of the very nature, the very meaning of our thinking. We can only think meaningfully about what lies on our side of that boundary. Due to the limitations of our creaturely thinking as a result of its subjection to the law, we can only engage in meaningless speculation when it comes to questions and pronouncements about whatever lies on the other side of the boundary. [18]

Taken by itself, this quotation could just as easily have come from the pen of Immanuel Kant. Only that which exists below the Boundary can be a subject for human investigation. The Boundary marks off the limits of what humans can know.

Unless qualified, the Dooyeweerdian's theory of the Boundary entails that it is impossible for any human being to think meaningfully about God. To be sure, Kalsbeek does add that we can think meaningfully about God as long as "we realize that we should limit ourselves to what God has revealed about himself to men."[19] But the problem that the Dooyeweerdians have raised for themselves is whether they have made the distinction between the human and divine minds so great that any revelation of truth becomes impossible. As we shall see later, a number of thinkers at the Institute for Christian Studies apparently embrace this position.

---

[18]L. Kalsbeek, *Contours of a Christian Philosophy*, pp. 74–75.
[19]Ibid., p. 75.

The Dooyeweerdians' rejection of the Logos doctrine is made clear in a recent paper by Al Wolters, a professor at the Institute for Christian Studies.[20] Wolters readily acknowledges the commitment of earlier Dutch Calvinists like Abraham Kuyper and Herman Bavinck to the Logos doctrine. In their epistemology, the ability to know was clearly dependent upon the Logos relationship between the divine mind and the human mind. Wolters is offended by that earlier commitment to the Logos doctrine and rejoices in the fact that the Amsterdam Philosophy of Dooyeweerd has rejected it.

For Wolters, rationality is totally below the Boundary. Logic, the principles of valid inference, do not apply beyond the Boundary; from which it follows that there is no continuity between the Creator and the creature. In Wolters' words, "There is no rational order that encompasses Creator and creation—not because the Creator is irrational, but because rationality is creature."[21] Wolters' comment raises two questions: Is not his position a clear denial of the image of God in humans? And how can anyone holding Wolters' position be confident that God is not irrational? The statement that God is not irrational purports to be a bit of knowledge about God. But Wolters' doctrine of the Boundary rules out any knowledge of the kind he has in mind when he seeks to assure his reader that God is not irrational.

The view of the Dooyeweerdians, then, is that there is no rational continuity between God and humanity. The motive of desiring to preserve the sovereignty and transcendence of God is laudatory, but the doctrine carries an extremely high price tag. It defends the divine transcendence by making God utterly unknowable. Any Christian who believes in the transcendence of God will have reached that conclusion as a result of some reasoning. The following argument represents one route by which many Christians reach that conclusion:

> If the Bible states that God is transcendent, then God is transcendent.
> The Bible says God is transcendent.
> Therefore, God is transcendent.

---

[20]Wolter's paper, as yet unpublished, entitled "Dutch Neocalvinism: Worldview, Philosophy and Rationality," was delivered in August, 1981 to a Toronto conference on "Rationality in the Calvinian Tradition."

[21]Ibid., Wolters, p. 12.

But according to Wolters and the other Dooyeweerdians, human reasoning can be valid only on the creature's side of the Boundary. No human reasoning can bring us to a knowledge of what is true beyond the Boundary. If human reason is only valid on this side of the Boundary, then any inference that God is transcendent must be an illegitimate application of human reason. What Alvin Plantinga wrote in connection with another type of theological agnosticism applies as well to the Amsterdam Philosophy; this kind of thinking about God

> begins in a pious and commendable concern for God's greatness and majesty and augustness; but it ends in agnosticism and in incoherence. For if none of our concepts apply to God [or if none of our inferences extend to God], then there is nothing we can know or truly believe of him—not even what is affirmed in the creeds or revealed in the Scriptures. And if there is nothing we can know or truly believe of him, then, of course, we cannot know or truly believe that none of our concepts apply to him. The view . . . is fatally ensnarled in self-referential absurdity.[22]

I shall have more to say about the Toronto Dooyeweerdians' view of Scripture in chapter 12.

CORNELIUS VAN TIL

One more evangelical thinker deserves comment in the context of this discussion. Cornelius Van Til, formerly professor of Christian apologetics at Westminster Theological Seminary, has influenced many in the Reformed tradition. It is well-known that Van Til for years held that a qualitative difference exists between the knowledge God has and that possessed by humans. God's knowledge and ours do not coincide at a single point.[23] But this implies, of course, that no proposition can mean the same thing to God and to humans. For twenty years or so, as a friendly critic of Van Til's views,[24] I have maintained that Van Til's

---

[22]Alvin Plantinga, *Does God Have A Nature?* (Milwaukee: Marquette University Press, 1980), p. 26.

[23]Van Til repeats this claim in most of his writings. One place to view it in action is his *A Christian Theory of Knowledge* (Philadelphia: Presbyterian and Reformed Publishing Co., 1969).

[24]See, for example, my books, *The New Evangelicalism* (Grand Rapids: Zondervan, 1963) and *The Philosophy of Gordon H. Clark* (Philadelphia: Presbyterian and Reformed Publishing Co., 1968), along with book reviews in the January 16, 1970 issue of *Christianity Today* (p. 349–50) and the July–August, 1980, issue of *Eternity* (p. 37).

position entails scepticism. As Gordon Clark has stated so well:

> If God knows all truths and knows the correct meaning of every proposition, and if no proposition means to man what it means to God, so that God's knowledge and man's knowledge do not coincide at any single point, it follows by rigorous necessity that man can have no truth at all. This conclusion is quite opposite to the views of Calvin . . . and undermines all Christianity. [25]

Only recently, however, have I come to understand that Van Til had developed his own version of the Dooyeweerdian Boundary between the human mind and the mind of God. To his credit, Van Til has not wavered from his earlier conviction that humans can have knowledge about God. Van Til has always contended earnestly for the doctrine of propositional revelation. His position has been that we can know only what God has explicitly revealed. I once asked Van Til if, when some human being knows that 1 plus 1 equals 2, that human being's knowledge is identical with God's knowledge. The question, I thought, was innocent enough. Van Til's only answer was to smile, shrug his shoulders, and declare that the question was improper in the sense that it had no answer. It had no answer because *any* proposed answer would presume what is impossible for Van Til, namely, that laws like those found in mathematics and logic apply beyond the Boundary. Van Til rejects the presumption that a person might know something about the mind of God that was not the product of special revelation. Unlike Van Til, few Christians have any difficulty affirming the following three propositions: (a) 1 plus 1 equals 2; (b) God knows that 1 plus 1 equals 2; and (c) when a human being knows that 1 plus 1 equals 2, his or her knowledge is identical with God's knowledge of the same proposition. It makes much more sense to reject the sceptical premises of Van Til's position than it does to deny any of these three claims.

At this point, of course, Van Til and his followers charge that my position entails a denial both of God's sovereignty and His incomprehensibility. The charge is ridiculous. Like Gordon Clark, I am not

---

[25]Gordon H. Clark, "Apologetics," in *Contemporary Evangelical Thought*, ed. Carl F. H. Henry (New York: Harper and Bros., 1957), p. 159.

moved by specious appeals to Scripture texts like Isaiah 55:8–9. Clark rejoins:

> Of course, the Scripture says God's thoughts are not our thoughts and his ways are not our ways. But is it good exegesis to say that this means his logic, his arithmetic, his truth are not ours? If this were so, what would the consequences be? It would mean not only that our additions and subtractions are all wrong, but also that all our thoughts, in history as well as in arithmetic, are all wrong. . . . To avoid such nonsense, which of course is a denial of the divine image . . . we must insist that truth is the same for God and man.[26]

While we obviously do not know everything, what we do know must be identical with what God knows. "God knows all truth, and unless we know something God knows, our ideas are untrue. It is absolutely essential therefore to insist that there is an area of coincidence between God's mind and our mind."[27] If this is denied, we are left not only without any knowledge of God, we are left without any knowledge at all.

As one might expect, it is difficult for anyone holding a position like Van Til's to be consistent. In A Christian Theory of Knowledge, Van Til warns that one must not take the biblical teaching about both divine sovereignty and human responsibility as a logical contradiction. On page 38 of the same book, he admits that the presence of a logical contradiction in the Bible would count as evidence against the Bible's claim to be the Word of God. In these passages, Van Til does what he himself says is impossible; he applies the law of noncontradiction on both sides of the Boundary.

In conclusion, one can ask how Van Til knows that no proposition can mean the same thing to God and to a human, that our knowledge and God's knowledge do not coincide at any point. This very knowledge claim says something about what lies beyond the Boundary. While the assorted rejections of logic found in the writings of Torrance, the followers of Dooyeweerd, and Van Til are (because of their sincere motives) pious nonsense, they are still nonsense.

---

[26]Gordon H. Clark, "The Axiom of Revelation," in The Philosophy of Gordon H. Clark, p. 76.

[27]Ibid.

Chapter 10

Reason
and
Religion

Although Aristotle was an empiricist in the sense that he believed knowledge of universals arose by abstraction from observation of particulars, he nevertheless made an important contribution to rationalism. He argued for a parallelism between thought, being, and language. One of rationalism's basic convictions is the belief that the world is rational. This means that a basic conformity exists between the structure of human reason and the structure of the world. Human reason, rationalists aver, is not involved in a struggle to understand a nonrational world. The laws that govern human thought are a reflection of the necessities that can be found in nature. Augustine certainly held this view: "The true nature of logical conclusions has not been arranged by men; rather they studied and took notice of it so that they might be able to learn or to teach it. It is perpetual in the order of things and divinely ordained."[1] For Augustine, the truth of propositions like "$2 + 2 = 4$" does not consist simply in the mental act of making this judgment. Rather, its truth lies in the eternal reality which makes the judgment true. The truths of logic are not empty tautologies devoid of any reference to being.

LOGIC AND REALITY

According to Aristotle, the laws of logic are not only laws of human thinking but also laws of reality with which one may grasp the actual logical structure of the world. Human language is sufficient to com-

---

[1] Augustine, *On Christian Doctrine* 2, 32, 50.

municate truth about both human reason and reality. The law of non-contradiction is a necessary principle of thought because it is first a necessary principle of being.

Aristotle defined the law of noncontradiction by stating that "the same attribute cannot at the same time belong and not belong to the same subject in the same respect."[2] In other words, "it is impossible that contrary attributes should belong at the same time to the same subject."[3] Aristotle realized that he could not demonstrate the truth of this law. But this was no cause for alarm. If argumentation is ever to begin, it must start by taking some things for granted. There are always some things that must be accepted without proof. In order for ultimate principles like the law of noncontradiction to be proved, they would either have to be deduced from other principles (in which case they would no longer be *ultimate*) or from themselves (in which case the supposed argument would be circular and not really a proof). Thus, any so-called proof of the law of noncontradiction would have to presuppose the truth of the law and would thus beg the question. But the lack of a direct proof for the law of noncontradiction is not a serious obstacle.

While no direct demonstration of the principle of noncontradiction exists, there is a most persuasive negative argument which can be put in the form of a dilemma. If the critic of the law says anything significant, then he must make use of the very law he is attempting to refute; and if he says nothing, then one need not worry about his opinions since he refuses to make them known. Aristotle was not demanding that his opponent say that something is or is not the case. He recognized that this would beg the question. All he asked was that his opponent say something significant for someone else as well as for himself. If he either says nothing or says that which has no meaning, he will be unable to reason.

The crucial part of the above argument was Aristotle's claim that significant speech was impossible apart from a tacit acceptance of the law of noncontradiction. This claim was one of two fundamental points that Aristotle wished to make concerning this logical principle. (1) On the linguistic level, contrary meanings may not (if one is to speak

---

[2]Aristotle, *Metaphysics*, tr. W. D. Ross (Oxford: Oxford University Press, 1908), 1005b, 18.

[3]Ibid., 1005b, 26.

intelligibly) be attributed to the same word at the same time and in the same sense; and (2) on the ontological level, contrary properties may not belong to the same subject at the same time and in the same sense.

Aristotle's position is clearly at odds with the position, so popular in much recent philosophy, that regards the law of noncontradiction as a purely formal law or as an arbitrary stipulation useful for constructing symbolic systems. Aristotle argued that the law has an ontological basis in reality. The law of noncontradiction is not simply a law of thought. It is a law of thought because it is first a law of being. Nor is the law something someone can take or leave. The denial of the law of non-contradiction leads to absurdity. It is impossible meaningfully to deny the laws of logic. If the law of noncontradiction is denied, nothing has meaning. If the laws of logic do not first mean what they say, nothing else can have meaning, including the denial of the laws.

Not only is significant thought and speech impossible if the law of noncontradiction is denied, significant human action also becomes impossible. Aristotle's statement of this point is classic:

> For why does a man walk to Megara and not stay at home thinking he is walking? Why does he not walk early some morning into a well or over a precipice, if one happens to be in his way? Why do we observe him guarding against this, evidently not thinking that falling in is alike good and not good? Evidently he judges one thing to be better and another worse. And if this is so, he must judge one thing to be man and another to be non-man, one thing to be sweet and another to be not-sweet.[4]

In other words, a denial of logic has consequences not only for epistemology and metaphysics, but for ethics as well. If all predications are true, there is no difference between walking to a nearby city and walking over a cliff; there is no difference between drinking milk and imbibing arsenic. But obviously there *is* a difference.

Because of the ontological status of the law of noncontradiction, contrary states of affairs are impossible. It is impossible, for example, that Socrates could be both man and non-man. Since the class of nonman is the complement of the class of man, the claim that Socrates

---

[4]Ibid., 1008b, 13–23.

is nonman is tantamount to saying that Socrates is everything else in the universe except man. Thus, anyone claiming that Socrates can be both man and nonman entails that Socrates can be a dog, star, tree, and indeed everything else in the universe. Gordon H. Clark outlines the implications:

> If contradictory statements are true of the same subject at the same time, evidently all things will be the same thing. Socrates will be a ship, a house, as well as a man; but then Crito will be a ship, a house, and a man. But if precisely the same attributes attach to Crito that attach to Socrates it follows that Socrates is Crito. Not only so, but the ship in the harbor, since it has the same list of attributes too, will be identified with this Socrates-Crito person. In fact, everything will be everything. Therefore everything will be the same thing. All differences among things will vanish and all will be one. [5]

This is only a sample of the nonsense that follows from any denial of the law of noncontradiction.

LOGIC AND LANGUAGE

Logic is as indispensable to language as it is to reality. Significant speech is impossible apart from an acceptance of the law of noncontradiction. If one is to speak intelligibly, contrary meanings may not be attributed to the same word at the same time and in the same sense. Since any refutation of the law of noncontradiction would have to be expressed in intelligible language and since significant speech presupposes the law, it is in principle impossible to deny the law. Anyone who objects to the principle must use the very principle he is attempting to refute.

> Now any given word must signify one thing, or a finite number of things, or an infinite number of things. If the word has a finite number of meanings, then it would be possible to invent a name for each meaning, so that all words would have a single meaning. But if each word has an infinite number of meanings, reasoning and conversation

---

[5]Clark, *Thales to Dewey*, p. 103.

> have become impossible because not to have one meaning
> is to have no meaning. But if a word has a meaning the
> object cannot be both man and not-man.[6]

If speech is to be intelligible, words must have univocal meanings. If "terms had an infinite number of meanings, then all reasoning would come to an end. For if a word is to convey a significance, it must not only mean something, it must also not mean something. If it had all the meanings of all the terms in the dictionary, it would be useless in speech."[7]

The fact that many words are ambiguous is irrelevant to this argument. As long as the possible meanings of a word are limited in number, one can always eliminate the ambiguity by assigning a different set of symbols to each meaning. For example, if, in the statement "S is P," P is ambiguous and has (let us say) five or six possible meanings, we may further specify "S is P_1," "S is P_2," and so on for each possible meaning. But if the law of noncontradiction is denied, there would then be no difference in meaning between P and non-P. Therefore, every word would have an infinite number of meanings. And if words have an infinite number of meanings, intelligible speech and reasoning becomes impossible. This is why the person who attempts to argue against the law of noncontradiction must make use of the very law he is trying to deny. In the now famous words of McTaggart, "No one ever tried to break logic but what logic broke him."[8]

LOGIC AND GOD

We have argued that the claim that there is a human logic that is different from God's logic is self-defeating and leads to nonsense. The

---

[6]Clark, *Christian View*, p. 292. One must not become confused at this point by the semantic matter of assigning different names to the same object. Jones may call a certain thing (x) a snark while Smith calls the same thing a krans. The question is not whether x can be a snark and nonsnark in name but in fact. Whatever x is called, its name ("snark") must not have an infinite number of meanings.

[7]Clark, *Thales To Dewey*, p. 100.

[8]A consideration of the varied attempts by contemporary philosophers to maintain that the laws of logic are only conventions or exercises in manipulating symbols according to certain rules is outside the scope of this book. An excellent critique of such positions can be found in Brand Blanshard's *Reason and Analysis* (La Salle, Illinois: Open Court Publishing Co., 1962). A brief but effective reply to the more recent attacks on the necessity of the law of noncontradiction by Willard Van Orman Quine is Carl R. Kordig's article, "Some Statements Are Immune To Revision," *The New Scholasticism* 55 (1981): 69–76.

law of noncontradiction is more than a law of human thinking; it is a fundamental law of being as well. It is a principle that is absolutely indispensable to significant thought, action, and speech. This extended discussion of the law of noncontradiction has implications for theology, and specifically for the crisis of revealed truth in contemporary theology. For if God is to communicate His thoughts to human beings, that communication must accord with the law of noncontradiction.

But does this constrain God? If so, or if not, what is the relationship between God and the necessary truths of logic? Plato, remember, made God subordinate to the Forms. Does the position taken in this book elevate logic above God? Not at all. God must not be made subordinate to any higher idea or principle, be it goodness, truth, unity, or logic. The laws of logic are not above God; they are not metaphysically ultimate. While reason is an attribute of God and thus uncreated, "it does not follow . . . that the laws of reason are independent of the will of God or in any way limit his power. The laws of reason may be taken as descriptive of the activity of God's will, and hence dependent on it though not created as the world has been created."[9]

How has sin affected human ability to reason? Has the combination of human finitude and sin made human reason completely defective? I think not. The scriptural doctrine of the image of God entails in part that humans possess a capacity for knowledge and rationality. But what effect has the Fall had on human reasoning powers? How did the Fall affect the cognitive functions of the image of God? Gordon Clark answers:

> The Fall seriously damaged God's image in man in all its parts. The intellect became depraved as well as the will. This is the doctrine of total depravity: no part or function of man is free from the effect of sin. However, the different functions are differently affected. While no act of will can be moral in the unregenerate man, it does not follow that no intellectual argument can be valid. . . . Therefore, in order not to assert that the image of God has been com-

[9]Clark, *Christian View*, p. 268. The subject of God's relationship to logic is explored in greater depth in Alvin Plantinga, *Does God Have A Nature?* (Milwaukee: Marquette University Press, 1980) and Ronald Nash, *The Concept of God* (forthcoming).

pletely annihilated, stress must be laid on its component of logic and reason.[10]

A careful distinction must be drawn between the noetic effect of sin on human mental *activity* and its effect on *subject matter*. The psychological activity of thinking a proposition to be true is subject to changing conditions of time. The fact of error in particular human judgments is one result of the noetic effect of original sin. But sin does not affect the truth of subject matter such as the multiplication tables. True propositions are universally true. Thus while sin may affect the psychological activity of thinking that a particular proposition is true or false, it does not affect the truth of falsity of that proposition. Sin may hinder the ability to reason correctly but it does not alter the laws of valid inference.

> Logic, the law of contradiction, is not affected by sin. Even if everyone constantly violated the laws of logic, they would not be less true than if everyone constantly observed them. Or, to use another example, no matter how many errors in subtraction can be found in the stubs of our checkbooks, mathematics itself is unaffected.[11]

Any theologian who claims that human rational powers are completely defective is in effect implying that among the multitude of things humans cannot know is the person of God. Furthermore, if we cannot know, then how do we know that we cannot know? Such a view reduces to scepticism and must be false. It is clear then that, in spite of original sin, we must be capable of knowing; and one of the things we can know is the laws of valid reasoning.

LOGIC AND FAITH

What is the relationship between logic and faith? Certainly it is not an inverse relation, as some contemporary theologians argue, insisting that the quotient of faith increases as its rational content decreases. The position of Thomas Aquinas is especially instructive in this connection. Aquinas (1225–1274) appeared on the scene at a time when many of his

---

[10]Gordon Clark, *The Philosophy of Gordon H. Clark*, ed. Ronald Nash (Philadelphia: The Presbyterian and Reformed Publishing Co., 1968), p. 75.

[11]Clark, *Christian View*, p. 299.

contemporaries believed that Christianity was threatened by the greatest intellectual challenge in its history. That threat, the philosophy of Aristotle, was first introduced into the Christian world about A.D. 1200. Even if Aristotle's philosophy had been properly understood and stated in accurate Latin translations, it would have been a potent challenge to medieval Christianity. But the Aristotelianism of the thirteenth century came complete with interpretations by Islamic philosophers, like Averroes (1126–1198), who confused a number of Aristotle's doctrines with those of certain Neoplatonists. Averroes' form of Aristotelianism rejected the doctrine of creation, denied personal survival after death, and placed numerous limitations on the extent of God's knowledge and power. Aristotelianism had previously been recognized as a threat to Islamic theology and charges of heresy within Islam had already been brought against adherents of these views. The Roman Catholic church of the Middle Ages sought to counteract the influence of these new and dangerous ideas by banning the teaching of certain elements of Aristotle's thought. But the ban was unsuccessful, especially at the University of Paris, where a group of Latin Averroists accepted Aristotle's philosophy as true even though they recognized its incompatibility with Christian doctrine.

During the thirteenth century, intellectuals in the Christian world took a variety of positions regarding the new philosophy. There were some who followed Averroes in proclaiming the supremacy of philosophy over revealed truth. These thirteenth-century forerunners of modern Christian liberals maintained that whenever a clear conflict between faith and reason arose, reason must always be accepted over faith. Others (the fundamentalists of their century, perhaps) insisted on the supremacy of faith. They argued that whenever revelation teaches one thing and Aristotle the opposite (regarding creation, for example), Aristotle must be rejected. In any conflict between the two, faith is to be preferred to reason. Still others appeared to maintain a double theory of truth. (Dare we call them the dialectical theologians of their age?) Siger of Brabant, for example, seems to have held that a proposition can be true in philosophy and its contradictory true in theology.

Paul Tillich often sounds like a twentieth-century Siger of Brabant. In his *Dynamics of Faith*, for example, Tillich insists that the meaning of truth for faith is something quite different from its meaning for science, history, and philosophy. As Tillich put it, "The truth of faith cannot be made dependent on the historical truth of the stories and legends in which faith has expressed itself. . . . [Nor can faith] be shaken by historical research even if its results are critical of the traditions in which the event is reported."[12] In other words, faith is immune from difficulties raised in science, history, and philosophy because it belongs to a different domain. Faith can rest in claims that are contradicted by competing claims in science, history, and philosophy.

To his credit, Aquinas would have no part of any of these moves to resolve the conflict between revelation and human claims to truth. Aquinas repudiated the double theory of truth. Two contradictory propositions, even if found in different areas like science and theology, cannot both be true at the same time and in the same sense. If Aristotle should prove to be correct about a certain belief which contradicts Scripture, the Christian should not hedge or hide behind a dubious theory of truth but be honest enough to admit that Scripture is wrong. But the Christian should also examine every alleged conflict between philosophy and theology. Perhaps the conflict is only apparent or perhaps it is the philosopher who is in error. Aquinas went even further and insisted that faith and reason, properly understood, can *never* really conflict. God's Word is true and what God teaches will always be consistent with whatever truth humans discover. The truth of faith and the truth of reason can never conflict logically.

CONCLUSION

It should now be clear how the Logos of God, the human logos, and the logos of the world fit together in one grand scheme that makes possible human knowledge of the world which God has created and the revelation of truth that God has communicated. Theories that deny this God-created interrelationship are not alternative theories of knowledge; they are theories that make knowledge impossible. There is no problem relating any so-called human reason to God. Reason and logic have cosmic significance. Reason has an intrinsic relationship to God. The law of noncontradiction is a law of being because the universe is the creation of a rational God. The rational world (the creation) is know-

---

[12]Paul Tillich, *Dynamics of Faith* (New York: Harper and Row, 1957), pp. 87, 89.

able because it is the projection of a rational God who objectifies His eternal thoughts in the creation. The mind of God can be known by the human logos because God has created us as creatures capable of such knowledge.

Chapter 11

Reason, Revelation and Language

In the introduction I argued that the modern assault on the possibility of human knowledge about God has been grounded on theories about the nature of God, the nature of human knowledge, and the nature of language. To this point, I have responded almost exclusively to the first two points. In this context, it is possible to give only an outline of my position on the nature of language. More complete statements of the theory can be found in Gordon Clark's *Religion, Reason and Revelation*[1] and in Carl Henry's *God, Revelation and Authority*.[2]

Theories about language are by-products of more general world views. This is certainly true of the several naturalistic theories of language around; it is equally true of theism. The Christian is entitled to develop a theory of language consistent with Christian presuppositons so long as that theory and its entailments do not conflict with the empirical data about language. One of the more important reasons why many contemporary theologians have given up on language as an adequate carrier of divinely revealed truth is their acceptance of presuppositions that are incompatible with a view of language that makes information about the transcendent possible.

CONTEMPORARY ASSUMPTIONS ABOUT LANGUAGE

The first of these assumptions is the belief that all language is incapable of expressing literal truth. An interesting fallacy is committed

---

[1]Gordon H. Clark, *Religion, Reason and Revelation* (Philadelphia: Presbyterian and Reformed, 1961), chapter 3.

[2]Carl F. H. Henry, *God, Revelation and Authority*, 3: 248–402.

by many proponents of this position. First, they point to the undeniable fact that all language is symbolic. From this fact, they infer that no language can be literally true. The specific error here goes by the name of the fallacy of equivocation, an error committed whenever a key word in an argument is used in two different senses. The word *symbolic* can mean either: (1) nonliteral or (2) that which serves as a symbol or representation for something else. It is undeniably (literally?) true that all language is symbolic in the second sense. But if the word *symbol* is used in the argument in question in this second sense, the conclusion does not follow. If "symbol" is used in the first sense, the conclusion does follow but the argument is trivial. That is, it simply states: all language is nonliteral; therefore, no language can be literal.

Language can serve a variety of functions. Many times, it is meant to be taken metaphorically or nonliterally. But the very possibility of nonliteral uses of language requires that there are also uses of language in which it is meant to be taken literally. If no language is capable of expressing literal truth, then, of course, it follows that even God cannot use language to communicate literal truth. But those who appeal to this argument conveniently ignore some of the fallout from their position. For example, if no language can be literally true, then it is also impossible for philosophers and theologians (including those who hold this position) to convey *their* thoughts in literally true propositions. Ironically, many of these writers act as if *their* sentences do convey literal truth.

The second alien presupposition is the claim that human language is derived from sensible human experience of the visible world. If this were true, it would be difficult to see how such a language could be adequate to express truth about a spiritual world and a transcendent being. Even if St. Paul, for example, had in some way received an intelligible revelation, how could he have communicated it to others? But before we get too excited about the supposed problem, we should look more carefully at the theory that gives rise to it.

As we saw in chapter 7, theories of knowledge may be either empiricist or rationalist. It is empiricism that gives rise to views of language that cannot account for the possibility of communication about nonsensible reality. How might the differences between rationalism and empiricism as theories of knowledge give rise to competing theories of language? One way to see this is to return to the model of the mind as a *tabula rasa* or blank tablet that was explained earlier. If the empiricist is correct and the human mind at birth is like a blank tablet, then in principle every feature of human language should be explicable in terms of what human beings acquire through their experiences of the world.

A RATIONALIST VIEW

The linguist Noam Chomsky is convinced that this cannot be done. He has received much attention for his rejection of empiricist and behaviorist accounts of the origin of language. His own view stresses the relationship between language and thought. Language, in his view, does not grow out of human experience. Instead, he maintains, language is made possible by human thought. "As far as we know," Chomsky writes, "human language is associated with a specific type of mental organization, not simply a higher degree of intelligence."[3]

One helpful way to approach Chomsky's theory* is to imagine a box with two openings marked respectively "input" and "output." Suppose that on a regular basis, far more leaves the box as output than enters the box. The natural conclusion to draw is that the additional output must result from what was already in the box to begin with. Chomsky believes the evidence clearly indicates that human language corresponds to his example of the box: far more comes out than ever goes in. Obviously, many features of a child's language are a direct output that results from information fed into the "box." But the actual use of language is far more complex than the accumulated total of input experience. Children learn the use of grammar very early in their lives. But their mastery of a grammar goes far beyond the sum total of things they have heard or learned. Children are soon able to speak and write new sentences unlike any they have heard or read. Thus, the actual use of language contains many characteristics that cannot be accounted for on the basis of stimulus and response.

---

[3]Noam Chomsky, *Language and Mind* (New York: Harcourt, Brace and World, 1968), p. 62.

*It should be clearly understood that in the argument that follows, I am not tying the view of language I espouse to the theories of Chomsky. I simply refer to Chomsky's well-known and highly respected views as one example of how a nonempiricist account of language might be formulated and how that type of formulation would relate to the position represented in this book.

When a human being uses language, far more is put out than sense experience ever put in. Human beings use grammar creatively. We are able to use and comprehend sentences unlike any heard or used in previous experience. In fact, most of the sentences we use and understand are new ones never encountered in prior experience. Chomsky believes this feature of language is explained by our possession of unconscious, innate knowledge of the rules of language. Returning to the box model, if output regularly exceeds input, the box must have contributed something. Chomsky concludes that the mind must contribute something to language learning. Because any particular grammar is able to generate an infinite number of new and different sentences, it must follow that knowledge of a language is the complex result of an interaction of input from one's environment and an innate structure of the human mind.[4]

Chomsky represents a rationalist approach to the theory of language; he stresses the primacy of mind and thought with respect to language building. The fundamental similarity of all human languages, Chomsky believes, suggests that the human brain contains an innate disposition to build grammar. Human beings come into the world already equipped with an innate ability to acquire and use language and to construct grammar. The principles of language are not acquired; they are present innately in every normal human mind at birth. Children utilize this innate knowledge when they learn the grammar of their own language. Language does not grow out of human experience. Instead, Chomsky maintains, language is made possible by human thought.

THE EMPIRICIST APPROACH

Basic to the empiricist approach to language is the belief that language like human knowledge arises from sense experience; language grows out of children's imitation of their parents' use of language. Since, on this view, words have their origin in sense experience, the original referent for any word must be something physical. Even words that denote relations are supposed to arise from an experience of spatial relations. Not surprisingly, advocates of such a theory of language conclude that human language cannot apply literally to things that are spiritual and nonspatial.

---

[4]For more on Chomsky's views, see Noam Chomsky, *Aspects of the Theory of Syntax* (Cambridge: MIT Press, 1965).

But we should pause and reflect a bit. All theologians use words like *soul* and *God* to refer to things that are spiritual and nonspatial. How can words that supposedly have an original physical referent suddenly refer adequately to something spiritual? Is it possible that some theologians have been too hasty in accepting an empiricist theory of language? "If all words are primarily physical or sensuous, and if relations are basically spatial, either language cannot properly apply to spiritual and nonspatial subjects, or one must explain how the physical meaning can be changed into a spiritual meaning. How can sensory experience give rise to words for soul and God?"[5] Carl Henry extends this critique:

> The prevalent contemporary theory that language originates in sense experience and represents a gradual evolutionary development of animal sounds is difficult to assess because its supposed stages have not been exhibited, and because there are striking differences between nonhuman utterances. Contrary to human language that communicates a descriptive content and changes from time to time and place to place, the sounds of birds and beasts are instinctive and constant, and can hardly be considered descriptive sentences. If words are primarily sensuous in their reference, as naturalism contends, and are not to be considered signs of a mental concept, nor to be correlated with intellection, then it should be emphasized that such explanation is not verified by the empirical criteria that naturalism cherishes.[6]

Karl Barth is an example of those theologians who regard human language as an unfit instrument to carry the truth of God. In his *Church Dogmatics*, he wrote: "The pictures in which we view God, the thoughts in which we think Him, the words with which we can define

---

[5]Clark, *Religion, Reason and Revelation*, p. 125.

[6]Henry, *God, Revelation and Authority*, 3:333. Henry agrees with Chomsky that the evolutionary theory that human language has evolved from animal noises is unproven. Such views have to distinguish between lower and more primitive stages where the animal uses noises and gestures to express emotion to higher stages where the sound actually becomes a vehicle of communicating thoughts. Advocates of the evolutionary hypothesis fail to establish a relation between the lower and higher states and do not really provide a mechanism by which the alleged passage from one level to another can take place. See Chomsky's *Language and Mind*, p. 60.

Him, are in themselves unfitted to this object and thus inappropriate to express and affirm the knowledge of Him."[7] This suspicion that words are generally unfit to carry anything as majestic as God's revelation is one element of the contemporary rejection of propositional revelation. Words themselves should never be regarded *as* God's revelation. At most, they can witness to the revelation; God may use words to "communicate" with human beings. But once again, the appearance of such views in a theologian who himself has written hundreds of thousands of words about God is more than a little ironic. Barth has told us that human language cannot be used to speak truly about God; God is simply too great for human language. What are we to make then of the thousands of sentences that Barth has written about God?

James Packer has drawn attention to several claims used by theologians like Barth to ground their scepticism about human language. (1) They assert that language is an inadequate instrument of human communication. But their view is obviously self-defeating. Consider the dilemma it raises for the person who holds this view. Either his own use of language is an exception to his claim or it is not. If his own language is an exception, then some uses of language can be an adequate instrument of human communication, in which case claim (1) is false. But if the proponent's own language is not an exception to his theory, his view can be safely ignored since on his own view he cannot possibly communicate that theory to us.

A second claim Packer identifies is that made by the theological sceptic who thinks that no human language can communicate information about transcendent reality. Few of the theologians who assert claim (2) practice what they preach. Any theologian who asserts (a) that human language cannot communicate information about the transcendent and (b) that God is transcendent is, of course, caught in a contradiction. The statement that God is transcendent is a communication about transcendent reality. Any advocate of claim (2) who wishes to be consistent must become dumb and forfeit forever the right to say anything about God. This is an interesting prospect to contemplate.

The third position that Packer finds in the thinking of those scepti-

---

[7]Karl Barth, *Church Dogmatics*, Vol. II: *The Doctrine of God*, ed. G. W. Bromiley and T. F. Torrance; tr. T. H. L. Parker, W. B. Johnston, H. Knight, and J. L. M. Haire (New York: Scribner, 1957), Pt. 1, p. 188.

cal about religious language is the denial that the language of Scripture is a propositional revelation of divine truth. Since we have already devoted two chapters to this unfortunate position, no further comment is needed except to note, with Packer, that the disjunction between personal and propositional revelation "makes God's method of self-disclosure analogous to the nonverbal communication of Harpo Marx."[8] As Packer continues:

> When leaders of theology thus decline to treat any of the statements of our thousand-plus-page, million-and-a-half word Bible as information from God to us and trumpet abroad that there can be no such thing as God-given information and that it is an intellectual mistake to look for any, it is no wonder if folk lose faith in the capacity of biblical speech to tell us facts about our Maker. Were we all clearheadedly logical, we should see ourselves as called by this situation to choose between such modern theologians . . . and such older ones as Moses and the prophets, Jesus Christ, Peter, Paul, John, and the author of Hebrews. Seeing the issue that way we might resolve that, on this point at least, we should ditch the moderns.[9]

What reasons are given to support the three claims just noted? Considering their significance, it is surprising to find hardly any. Modern theologians seem to regard these claims as self-evident, so that no support is really needed. That confidence is unwarranted. The truth seems to be that no support can be given.

What theory of language do I offer in lieu of the basically empiricist position that grounds the prevailing scepticism toward language as a vehicle of divine revelation? My alternative view flows naturally from my acceptance of a Logos epistemology: The omnipotent God has created human beings as rational creatures who possess innately the capacity to think and to use language. Language is possible because humans, created in the image of God, possess innately a priori categories of thought and the ability to use and understand language. As Carl Henry explains,

---

[8]James I. Packer, "The Adequacy of Human Language" in *Inerrancy*, ed. Norman L. Geisler (Grand Rapids: Zondervan, 1980), p. 205.
  [9]Ibid.

> Since every mind is lighted by the Logos or Reason of God,
> thought stands behind language. . . . Man's ability to think
> and to speak [is] God-given for certain essential
> purposes—for receiving a verbal revelation, for approaching
> God in prayer, and for conversing with other men about
> God and spiritual realities. . . . The gift of human speech
> and language, in brief, presupposes the *imago Dei*, par-
> ticularly rationality. [10]

Humans can communicate only when they share the same ideas.
"The situation," Gordon Clark says, "is somewhat like that of cryptog-
raphers who can break any cipher. The symbols are at first unknown;
but because the ideas expressed are common, the message can be understood. If language had no thought behind it, as the behaviorists
claim, and if the symbols were just a random aggregate of marks, there
would be no cipher to break."[11] Therefore, the sufficiency of human
language to communicate truth about a transcendent God rests on "the
theomorphism of created man, whom God made a language user, able
to receive God's linguistic communication and to respond in kind."[12]

Basic to the Christian world view is the presupposition that the
human being is a creature who carries the image of God. Essential to
this image is rationality, a rationality that reflects the rationality of God's
own mind. Human language is adequate as a vehicle for divine revelation and for human communication about God because it is a divinely
given instrument. God can therefore reveal truth about Himself
through words. Thought exists behind language as its necessary condition. Communication is possible because the human creatures using
language are enlightened by the divine Logos, are in possession of
certain innate ideas.

---

[10]Henry, *God, Revelation and Authority*, 3: 389–90.
[11]Clark, *Religion, Reason and Revelation*, p. 135.
[12]Packer, p. 219.

Chapter 12

Revelation and the Bible

Until recently, regardless of how much they may have disagreed on other points, Evangelicals have shared the common conviction that God had revealed truth about Himself in Holy Scripture. This traditional consensus about revelation no longer exists. The current disagreement among Evangelicals concerning the relationship between revelation and the Bible is due, in part, to the presence of Hume's Gap and Kant's Wall in contemporary evangelical thought. In this final chapter I will address this central issue directly.

This task is hindered, however, by several obstacles. Many who, in personal conversation or classroom teaching, avow their opposition to propositional revelation have not expressed their doubts in print. Secondly, from the writings of those who have published their views, it is clear that they are rejecting a mere stereotype of propositional revelation. As caricatured by those who reject it, the doctrine of propositional revelation is an unrecognizable position held by no one that I know. A third problem encountered in any attempt to explore contemporary evangelical attitudes towards these issues is the extremely ambiguous way in which the opponents of propositional revelation formulate their own alternative. And, finally, effective dialogue on these topics is impeded by the fact that few of the participants seem to recognize the centrality of the Logos doctrine to the debate. The issues of the debate could be set forth much more clearly if participants would clarify their stance toward the Logos doctrine.

This chapter will begin by noting a few examples of Evangelicals who appear to reject the doctrine of cognitive revelation. Because I am more concerned, however, about Evangelicals who stop short of such an extreme position and aver (confusedly, I think) some kind of cognitive revelation, most of the chapter will focus on Evangelical Donald Bloesch. Author of the important two-volume work *Essentials of Evangelical Theology*, Bloesch is representative of a group of Evangelicals who, because they reject the Logos doctrine and have no real confidence in God's ability to communicate propositional truth to the human mind, give an extremely fuzzy treatment of the relation between revelation and the Bible. Since Bloesch has discussed the relation between revelation and Scripture in detail and since his position is similar to that of other Evangelicals who declare their opposition to propositional revelation, an examination of his view is a helpful way of understanding what many other Evangelicals have tried to say.

DUTCH AND CANADIAN CALVINISM

The most explicit renunciations of cognitive revelation by contemporary Evangelicals have come from people associated with The Institute for Christian Studies in Toronto. James Olthuis of ICS, for example, has stated that the Bible is "not the Word of God period." Olthuis views Scripture as only "redemptive concentrations of the Word of God."[1] Arnold DeGraaff, another ICS professor, has written that "you distort the Scriptures when you read them as a collection of objective statements about God and man, as truths in propositional form, or a collection of moral lessons. They do not contain any rational, general theological statements about God and his creation, from which we can deduce some moral applications."[2] Still another ICS professor, Hendrick Hart, insists that the Bible should not be reduced "to a set of truths, a collection of infallible propositions."[3] In the same book, Hart states that "the Bible is not the Word of God at all but is only an authoritatively inspired instance . . . of God's

---

[1]The Olthuis quotes come from an unpublished paper delivered at Calvin College. They are cited by Hary L. Downs in his book, *The Distinction between 'Power-Word' and 'Text-Word' in Recent Reformed Thought* Nutley, New Jersey: Presbyterian and Reformed, 1974), p. 102.

[2]Arnold DeGraaff and Calvin Seerveld, *Understanding the Scriptures* (Hamilton, Ontario: Guardian Press, 1968), p. 2.

[3]Hendrick Hart, *The Challenge of Our Age* (Hamilton, Ontario: Guardian Press, 1968), p. 119.

Word-revelation."[4] Hart's comments continued an earlier attack on the view that Scripture is objective revelation in an article written for *Sola Fide*. He maintained that

> the Bible is a collection of writings, of which we confess that they are so inspired by God that under the guidance of his Spirit they are to us a completely reliable, unified, trustworthy witness to his Word, an infallible revelation of that Word. These writings are not that Word, they reveal it. Because of this revelational character, this relation to the Word, this being relative to the Word, we may call the Bible in an analogical sense, the Word of God. . . . The Bible is not to be identified with the Word of God. . . . The Word of God . . . is not a book at all.[5]

It is difficult to see precisely how Hart's separation of the Bible and the Word of God differs from the neo-orthodox position represented by Emil Brunner. The ICS view of the Bible has come under attack from other Calvinists, especially faculty members at Westminster Theological Seminary.[6]

The well-known Dutch theologian, G. C. Berkouwer, has also received considerable attention for what is perceived to be a vacillating attitude toward the Scriptures.[7] Gordon R. Lewis laments the extent to which, in his later writings on Scripture, Berkouwer capitulates to Barthian emphases. According to Lewis, "in Berkouwer's doctrine of special revelation, there is no objective scriptural content that is identified with the Word of God. The Bible remains merely a time-bound human witness to Christ."[8] Henry Krabbendam reports on the growing influence of Barth on Berkouwer's understanding of Scripture.

> Warfield and the early Berkouwer hold that Scripture is the Word of God in the sense that the human words as God-breathed are a divine product. As such they are true,

---

[4]Ibid., p. 131. In ICS circles, "Word-revelation" means something distinct from the Bible.

[5]Hendrick Hart, "Can The Bible be an Idol?" *Sola Fide*, Sept., 1964, pp. 9–10.

[6]Some of the details of this debate can be traced in the book by Harry Downs, already cited.

[7]The criticisms are directed primarily against Berkouwer's later work, *Holy Scripture* (Grand Rapids: Eerdmans, 1975).

[8]Gordon R. Lewis, "The Human Authorship of Inspired Scripture" in *Inerrancy*, ed. Norman L. Geisler (Grand Rapids: Zondervan, 1979), p. 248.

trustworthy, infallible, inerrant, and authoritative in every pronouncement they make, in every subject matter they address, and in every area in which they speak—as well as being fit to be the means of regeneration, justification, and sanctification. The later Berkouwer holds that Scripture is the word of man in the same sense in which every other human document is the word of man. At the same time, it is nevertheless in the act of faith proclaimed by the apostles and confessed by the church as the God-breathed Word of God by virtue of its witness to Christ.[9]

According to Krabbendam, the later Berkouwer (the Berkouwer who wrote *Holy Scripture*) is struck by the mystery "that God uses a fallible book to convey a divine message. Berkouwer is forced to refer to this as a mystery because the realm of revelation and faith is not continuous with that of the written or spoken word."[10]

Some would question this evaluation by Lewis and Krabbendam. But Berkouwer's ambiguity leaves the issue open. As Geoffrey Bromiley said in his review of Berkouwer's *Holy Scripture*, it would do Berkouwer "a serious injustice to say that he personally espouses a compromising view [of Scripture]. The problem remains, however, that his presentation opens up unhappy possibilities that his many imprecise or ambivalent statements in no way exclude."[11]

DONALD BLOESCH

From Dutch and Canadian Calvinism, we turn to the views of Donald Bloesch. Bloesch is an important evangelical resource. He has already produced a number of influential books in addition to his systematic theology, *Essentials of Evangelical Theology*. Much of what Bloesch says in his account of the Bible is sound. He is certainly correct when he urges Evangelicals to recognize the importance of attaining some creedal identity:

---

[9]Henry Krabbendam, "B. B. Warfield Versus G. C. Berkouwer on Scripture," in *Inerrancy*, p. 438.

[10]Ibid.

[11]*Christianity Today*, November 21, 1975, p. 45. David Wells made a similar point in his review: "It would be easy to charge Berkouwer with positing a dichotomy between truth as it relates to faith and truth as it relates to the spatio-temporal world; whether it would be fair to do this is another matter." *Journal of the Evangelical Theological Society*, 19 (1976): 60.

> On the one hand, we have creedal churches that merely recite creeds handed down from tradition, and, on the other, there are creedless churches that languish in a doctrinal vacuum. . . . Our need is for a confessing church that will boldly confront a secularized world with the claims of the Gospel. Confessions should not be straight-jackets; yet at the same time they should be more than just general guides. An authentic confession, one that derives its inspiration from Scripture, is a norm for faith, though not an absolute norm. It is a test as well as a testimony of faith, but it does not base the case for the faith on human formulation alone but on fidelity to a living Lord.[12]

Bloesch is also correct in his insistence on the primacy of Scripture over religious experience and feelings.[13] Holiness denominations that encourage or allow their followers to place their private visions, dreams, and feelings on a par with Scripture need to give more attention to the dangers resident in such a practice.

Unfortunately, Bloesch's overall doctrine of Scripture is a major disappointment. While Bloesch does not deny that revelation is, among other things, a communication of truth, his system leaves no room for the Logos doctrine and its teaching of a fundamental relationship between the human and divine minds that alone can ground the communication of divine truth. For Bloesch, the Bible is the Word of God only in an *indirect* sense. That is, the Bible is the Word of God only when it is actually used by the Holy Spirit as an instrument of God's speaking. Bloesch refuses "to posit an absolute equation between the letter of the Bible and divine revelation."[14] Rather, he maintains, the words of Scripture are a medium "by which we hear and know the living Word."[15]

Bloesch realizes that, left unqualified, these words could mislead readers and suggest that he holds a view that is essentially the same as that held by neo-orthodox thinkers like Emil Brunner. Consequently, Bloesch seeks to distinguish his position from neo-orthodoxy. He points

---

[12]Donald G. Bloesch, *Essentials of Evangelical Theology*, 2 vols. (San Francisco: Harper and Row, 1979), 2: 280.

[13]Bloesch, *Essentials*, 1: 60ff.

[14]Ibid., 1: xi.

[15]Ibid.

out, for example, that, like the incarnate Christ, Scripture has both a human and a divine side. This he gives as a reason to refuse (as he does) to equate the words of the Bible and the Word of God. Liberals erred, he continues, when they ignored the divine side to Scripture and treated it as a wholly human book, just as they tended to deny the deity of Jesus. But too often, conservatives err in the other direction by exalting the divine side of Scripture and ignoring its human dimension. As Bloesch sees it, "the Bible is not partly the Word of God and partly the word of man: it is in its entirety the very Word of God and the very word of man."[16] Conservative Christians believe that Jesus is both fully human and fully God, even though the doctrine of the two natures of Christ raises some difficult questions. Since Evangelicals are used to wrestling with the difficulties that arise from their belief in the two natures of Christ, they should not draw back from a belief in the dual nature of Scripture simply because that view raises a few problems of its own.

But Bloesch's efforts do not persuade. His view of Scripture is defective not because he is more honest than other Evangelicals in acknowledging the human dimension of Scripture, but because some control-beliefs borrowed from Barth continue to lurk in the shadows of his theory. Consider the following:

> Revelation is better spoken of as polydimensional rather than propositional in the strict sense, in that it connotes the event of God speaking as well as the truth of what is spoken: this truth, moreover, takes various linguistic forms including the propositional. Objective intelligible truth is revealed (though not exhaustively), but the formulation in the Bible is one step removed from this truth even while standing in continuity with it. The truth of revelation can be apprehended through the medium of the human language *which attests it*, but only by the action of the Spirit.[17]

Except for the last sentence, I could have written this paragraph myself. Bloesch and I agree that revelation can communicate objective intelligible truth. No informed Christian should have any problem with the qualification that the truth God reveals is never exhaustive. But

---

[16]Ibid., 1: 52.
[17]Ibid., 1: 78; italics mine.

why, considering all the words Bloesch might have used, does he use the weak term *attest*? Why is he content to say only that the language of Scripture *attests* the truth of revelation? What prevents him from selecting one of several stronger verbs and saying that the language of Scripture actually *expresses* God's revelation? At the end of the paragraph Bloesch suggests that the language of Scripture only *becomes* revelation when it is energized by the action of the Holy Spirit. In my discussion of revelation in chapter 4, I explicitly rejected an exclusively static account of divine revelation and moved in the direction of a dynamic view of revelation in which *both* the written word and the work of the Spirit are vital. But in my view, revealed truth is still revelation even when no one is aware of it. (This is the point of my story of the lost letter that revealed the truth about the relationship between the mother and the lost son.) Bloesch apparently does not want to say this and, consequently, stays dangerously close to neo-orthodoxy. He seems to say that when the words of Scripture are not accompanied by the work of the Holy Spirit, it is impossible for Scripture to be revelation: "The truth of revelation can be apprehended only by faith."[18]

Both Berkouwer and Bloesch maintain that Word and Spirit are inseparable. One of the problems in sorting out an adequate theory of revelation is clarifying what this claim means. It is comparatively easy to repeat this claim in a seminary classroom. But in the laboratory of life, it often appears as though Word and Spirit are separated. Many people have read the Bible, understood its meaning, believed the statements to be true and yet failed to receive the spiritual impact of the words. Bloesch's position seems to entail the impossibility of a person's being an unregenerate inerrantist, that is, someone who accepts all Scripture as divinely revealed truth who is at the same time devoid of saving faith. Has Bloesch never met someone like this: Søren Kierkegaard certainly did. Kierkegaard seems to have believed that most of the citizens of the Denmark of his day fell into this category. Even though they may have been baptized members of the Lutheran Church and knew the objective truth about Christianity and accepted the Bible as revealed truth, they were not really Christians. My own youth was spent in a denomination very much like the one Kierkegaard knew. But Bloesch apparently be-

---

[18]*Essentials*, 2: 293, n. 33.

lieves this common state of affairs is impossible. For him, the moment any person apprehends anything in the Bible as revealed truth, that person must also be a recipient of special grace.

Does Bloesch really hold this view? In volume 2 of his systematic theology, he writes: "The Bible is the Word of God in all that it teaches, though this teaching is not immediately self-evident but must be unveiled by the Spirit."[19] Elsewhere in the same volume, he claims that apart from special grace, an "outsider" cannot understand one single item of revelation.[20] These are strong statements which, when taken literally, easily suggest counter-examples. Consider the first verse of the Bible. Many people understand and believe the Genesis claim that God is Creator of heaven and earth even though they have not experienced the new birth. A person does not have to become a Christian believer to understand and believe Genesis 1:1. As for Bloesch's conviction that no truth in Scripture is immediately self-evident unless unveiled by the Holy Spirit, consider 2 Samuel 5:3–4: "So all the elders of Israel came to the king at Hebron . . . and they anointed David king over Israel. David was thirty years old when he began to reign, and he reigned forty years." The meaning of this text is patently self-evident: David was thirty years old when he became king and he ruled for forty years. In the light of a passage like this, how are we to understand Bloesch's claim that the teaching of Scripture "is not immediately self-evident but must be unveiled by the Spirit"?

A basic fault of Bloesch's treatment of Scripture is his continual confusion of two different senses of truth. It is difficult to find any place in his discussion of revelation and the Bible where Bloesch concedes that a particular statement in Scripture is true (and revelational) if it is not also salvational. Clearly something happens to the truths of Scripture when the Holy Spirit uses them to convict of sin, righteousness, and judgment; something happens when an unregenerate mind is enlightened and an unregenerate heart opened to receive the truth of God. But does this mean that the passage was not true prior to this regeneration? Does this mean that biblical texts (like Genesis 1:1 and 2 Samuel 5:3–4) that have no clear salvational relevance are not true or that they are not revelation? Surely Bloesch does not intend to answer either

[19]Ibid., 2: 273.
[20]Ibid., 2: 268.

question in the affirmative. But much that he writes suggests that non-salvational Scripture is not revelation.

Suppose we concede the common sense distinction between a truth and a *saving* truth. An example of a plain and simple truth might be the statement that David became king at the age of thirty. It is difficult to see how this true statement could also become a saving truth. An example of a saving truth could presumably be a verse like Romans 10:9 or John 3:16. It is relatively easy to see how such verses could, for some people, be examples only of our first type of truth. For Romans 10:9 or John 3:16, while true, can only become saving truths when the Holy Spirit applies the truth to the heart and life of the agent. My problem with Bloesch does not concern his treatment of verses like John 3:16; it is what he does with the rest of the Bible that is troubling.

What then is Bloesch's reaction to the claim that *God can reveal truth in a nonsalvational sentence?* Based upon everything he has written thus far, Bloesch appears to reject it. But the implications of this rejection are rather far-reaching. For one thing, Bloesch's position suggests that verses like "David became king at the age of thirty" are either not true or not revelation. It seems likely that Bloesch would reject these entailments. But if so, some modifications of his doctrine of revelation seem in order. From the true premise that no one can have a saving understanding of the Bible apart from the redemptive work of the Holy Spirit, Bloesch draws the invalid conclusion that no one can understand *anything* revealed in Scripture apart from the redemptive work of the Holy Spirit. It is possible that the apparent confusions in Bloesch's account of revelation are a product of a tension in his system; this tension results from Bloesch's desire to develop a view of Scripture that avoids the errors of neo-orthodoxy while maintaining a fatal commitment to an epistemology according to which God cannot communicate truth to the human mind in human language.

BLOESCH'S CRITIQUE OF OTHER VIEWS

Based on Bloesch's own positive statements, it is difficult to discover precisely what he thinks of the relationship between revelation and Scripture. Perhaps the picture will become more clear if we examine his criticism of those with whom he disagrees. He certainly does not want his position confused with that of neo-orthodoxy. As he puts it, "in left-wing neo-orthodoxy, revelation is dissolved in an existential encounter." In other words, he is saying, do not confuse me with Tillich, Bultmann, or even Brunner. But on the other hand, "in right-wing scholastic orthodoxy, revelation is frozen into a propositional formula."[21] Who does he have in mind here? From various references, "right-wing scholastic orthodoxy" seems to include the proponents of propositional revelation. But notice how he explains their view: "revelation is frozen into a propositional formula." Does anyone today actually hold such a static view of revelation? Anything is possible, I suppose. But as I have attempted to show throughout this book, the position Bloesch describes is not that held by those, like myself, who advocate belief in propositional revelation.

Bloesch claims to be seeking a middle ground between two positions that serve as foils for his own: Brunner and the mystics on the one side and those he identifies as evangelical rationalists on the other. Bloesch rejects Brunner's view because Brunner represents a totally dynamic view of revelation; while the evangelical rationalists are rejected for advancing a static view of revelation. Bloesch wants a theory of revelation that mediates between the static and the dynamic, between the objective and the subjective. But that is also a goal of this book. Where then do we differ? Bloesch and I certainly differ in our understanding of and our appraisal of evangelical rationalism. Bloesch represents it as holding a totally static view of divine revelation. I think his account is a caricature. We also differ in our willingness to make accommodations to a dynamic view of revelation along Barthian lines. Perhaps some Evangelicals have overreacted to what they understand to be an emphasis on the dynamic in some theories of revelation. But it appears that thinkers like Berkouwer and Bloesch have been so anxious to correct what they have taken to be a static view of revelation (the dead letter of the Word), that they have overexaggerated the dynamic element. In spite of all that Berkouwer and Bloesch have said about Word and Spirit being inseparable, they tend to exalt Spirit *over* Word; they imply that the Word is nothing apart from the Spirit. Attaining the proper balance between objective and subjective, Word and Spirit, is the problem. But that balance is hardly possible in the presence of

---

[21]Ibid., 2: 273.

claims that no biblical statement can be revealed truth in the absence of the saving work of the Holy Spirit.

Bloesch's basic error is simple: he confuses the difference between truth and the apprehension of truth. Imagine that some great and learned teacher lectures to a group of college freshmen on some extremely technical subject. Suppose as well that that lecture is recorded on tape. Imagine also that no one in the class understands what the teacher says. Suppose finally that many years later some of those former students return for a reunion and, by chance, listen anew to the taped lecture that none of them understood when they were freshmen. This time the lecture *is* understood. Each of the listeners marvels at how brilliant and clear the words now seem. How would Bloesch analyze this situation if he were to apply his understanding of Scripture to it? Bloesch would have to say that because the teacher's words were not understood during their first delivery, they were not true; by analogy to Scripture, we might say they were not revelation. Only much later, when the very same words were understood did they *become* true. But, as I have suggested, this is to mistake an unprepared audience for an untrue message. It confuses truth with apprehension of truth. It makes much more sense to recognize that the teacher's words were true all the time; they were true when delivered even though not understood; and they were still true years later when the audience, now properly prepared, finally understood them.

What is the sum of all this! So far, the effort by Evangelicals like Bloesch to develop a mediating view of Scripture and revelation is a losing proposition. It fails to go far enough. It falls at least one giant step short of what is required. And what is required is simply to remember that while there is nothing to be gained by withholding the property of revealed truth from the inscripturation of God's Word in the Bible, there is a great deal to be lost. Bloesch and others seem to dismiss this insight. Without it, a balanced view of revelation becomes impossible since there is nothing left to balance.

CONCLUSION

My accounts of rationalism, the Logos, logic, and language fit together into one package. A blank mind (*tabula rasa*) cannot know anything; human knowledge of anything depends upon an a priori possession of innate categories of thought. These categories are ours by virtue of having been created in God's image, a fact that guarantees that the human structure of reasoning matches the divine reason. Reason subsists in the mind of God eternally. Reason also characterizes the human mind. And reason is objectified in the world because of its relation to the divine Logos. Language is a divinely-given gift to facilitate a communion between God and humans that is both personal and cognitive. Evangelicals have good reason therefore to protest the "needless relinquishment of cognitive knowledge of the spiritual world"[22] that is such a prominent feature of contemporary theology. Any flight from reason and of logic is a flight from reality. All who repudiate logic automatically cut themselves off from any possible knowledge of God and His creation. The Word of God (that includes revealed information from God and of God) is not alien to the human mind. Neither the nature of God nor the nature of human knowledge and language preclude the possibility of the human mind attaining cognitive knowledge of the Word of God.

---

[22]Carl F. H. Henry, "Reply to the God-Is-Dead Mavericks," *Christianity Today* 10 May 27, 1966, p. 894.

Index of Names

◆

Index of Subjects

◆

135